Chinese Astrology

MAN-HO KWOK
and MARTIN PALMER

Chinese Astrology

FORECAST YOUR FUTURE FROM YOUR CHINESE HOROSCOPE

REDFeather

MIND | BODY | SPIRIT

An Imprint of Schiffer Publishing

"Red Feather Mind Body Spirit" logo is a registered trademark of Schiffer Publishing, Ltd.
Published by Red Feather Mind, Body, Spirit
An imprint of Schiffer Publishing, Ltd.
4880 Lower Valley Road
Atglen, PA 19310
Phone: (610) 593-1777; Fax: (610) 593-2002
E-mail: Info@schifferbooks.com
Web: www.schifferbooks.com

Library of Congress Control Number: 2018939473

First published in Great Britain in 1997 by Blandford.

ISBN: 978-0-7643-5594-3

Printed in China

CONTENTS

THE JADE EMPEROR AND THE TWELVE ANIMALS

This story reveals how the Jade Emperor, the ruler of heaven, decided which animals to choose and the order of importance in which they should be placed.

The Jade Emperor ruled the heavens and all they contained but he had never been to earth, and he wondered about the shapes and colors of all its creatures. One day he summoned his chief adviser.

"I have ruled for many years," said the Emperor, "but I have never seen these strange animals. What do they look like? I want to see their features and characteristics; I would like to observe the way that they move and hear the sounds that they make. How intelligent are they, and how do they help humanity?"

The adviser told him that there were thousands of earthly creatures – some walked, others flew, some crawled and others slithered. It would take many months to gather examples of each and present them. Did his majesty want to see them all?

"No, I shall waste too much time. Select the twelve most interesting animals and bring them to me so I can grade them according to color and shape."

The adviser thought of all the animals he knew and decided to send an invitation to the rat, and told him, in turn, to give an invitation to his friend the cat. Further invitations were sent to the ox, the tiger, the rabbit, the dragon, the snake, the horse, the ram, the monkey, the rooster and the dog, asking them to present themselves before the Emperor at six o'clock the following morning.

The rat was proud to receive this invitation and immediately set off to reveal the good news to the cat. The cat was also overjoyed but, afraid that he might oversleep, made the rat promise to wake him in time. That night the rat pondered on how handsome and sleek the cat was and how ugly he would appear in comparison. He decided that the only way to prevent the cat taking all the praise was to let him oversleep the following morning.

At six o'clock, eleven animals lined up before the Jade Emperor, who slowly inspected them. When he came to the end of the line he turned to his adviser.

"They are all interesting but why are there only eleven animals?"

The adviser had no answer but quickly sent a servant down to earth to catch the first animal he saw and bring it back to heaven. The servant arrived on a country road and saw a farmer carrying a pig to market.

"Please stop," entreated the servant, "I need your pig now! The Jade Emperor wants to see this creature immediately. Think of the honor of displaying this pig to the ruler of heaven."

The farmer was duly impressed by the servant's news and so he handed over his pig, which was then carried off to the parade.

Meanwhile, the rat was afraid he would go unnoticed and so he jumped on the ox's back and began to play a flute. The Emperor was so charmed by this unusual animal that he gave him first place. The Jade Emperor then gave the ox second place, since he had been generous enough to let the rat sit on his back. The tiger looked courageous and was given third place, and the rabbit, because of his fine white fur, was given fourth place. The Emperor thought the dragon looked like a powerful snake with legs, and so he placed him fifth. The snake was sixth because of his curving, sinuous body, the horse seventh because of his elegant bearing, and the ram eighth because of his strong horns.

The monkey was agile and alert so was given ninth place, the rooster had such fine feathers he was tenth, and the watchful and protective dog was given eleventh place. The pig stood at the end of the line; he may not have been as interesting as the others but he had made the effort to be there and was allowed the final place.

When the ceremony had finished, the cat came running into the palace and begged the Emperor to consider him, but it was too late – the animals had been chosen. When the cat saw the rat standing in first place he chased him with intent to kill. This is why, even today, a cat and rat cannot be friends.

INTRODUCTION

Astrology is one of the most ancient Chinese arts. For centuries it has been influential in the lives of the Chinese, from emperors to peasants. Today it no longer plays a role in affairs of state, and yet it still absorbs the interest of millions of people all over the world.

The history of astrology can be traced back thousands of years to a time when the arts of astrology and astronomy were the same. Astronomers observed the order and movement of the stars to see what heaven was planning for earth, and up to the twentieth century both astronomers and astrologers were respected officials at the Imperial Court. The Chinese almanac or *T'ung Shu*, which is still produced every year, lists astrological and astronomical data for each day of the Chinese year. Using the guidance in the *T'ung Shu*, many decide which are the auspicious days to open a business, marry, embark on a long journey or make other personal decisions.

The first reference to a yearly calendar dates back more than 4,000 years and tells how Emperor Yao commanded the astronomers Hsi and Ho to calculate a calendar so the people would know when the seasons began and therefore when to plant and sow. The Emperor could then decree the dates for the seasons and participate in the rituals that marked events of the agricultural year. Gradually, the calendar began to be consulted to decide on dates for important matters of state or to divine the fortunes of the emperors. Another 2,000 years passed before astrology was applied to individual fortunes. The popularity of personal readings based on astrology soon started to grow, and by the T'ang dynasty (618–907 CE) an encyclopedia had been constructed around the art of fortune-telling. Since that time astrology has been part of everyday life for many of the Chinese.

THE TWELVE ANIMALS AND THE SIXTY-YEAR CYCLE

Although the twelve animals are the most popular and familiar aspect of Chinese astrology in the West, they are just one aspect of the Chinese system of counting the years. Chinese time is measured by a cycle of sixty years, and this cycle is formed by the interaction of astrological features known as Heavenly Stems and Earthly Branches. These pair up to give sixty different combinations over a sixty-year period, and then the cycle begins all over again (this is discussed further in Chapter Three). In turn, they are also linked to days and hours, and to the twelve animals, and therefore your Heavenly Stem and Earthly Branch also have an influence on your character and your fortune. And they are used in the more unusual "Three Lives" system, based on readings traditionally made by a traveling fortune-teller at the birth of a child (see "Using This Book," opposite).

THE LUNAR CALENDAR

The lunar calendar is calculated according to the phases of the moon, in contrast to the Western calendar, which is calculated according to the orbit of the earth around the sun. The lunar year has twelve moons, and each moon lasts for just over twenty-nine and a half days. In order to make the days in each moon full days, there are six "small" months, which have twenty-nine days each, and six "large" months, which have thirty days each, making a total of 354 days, eleven days short of the solar calendar.

Occasionally, the length of the Chinese years changes and there may be either seven "small" months (a total of 353 days), or sometimes seven "large" months (a total of 355 days). As each year passes, the lunar calendar usually falls short of the solar year by ten to twelve days; so in order to bring the lunar calendar in line with the solar calendar an extra month is added at roughly three-year intervals. These months follow the month they are linked with; for example, in 1987 the extra month was month six and followed the normal month six. The lunar chart at the back of the book lists the dates for all the lunar months, and also shows you how to find out your lunar day of birth. You will need to know this information in order to work out a number of the readings included in this book.

USING THIS BOOK

Each chapter features a different aspect of your horoscope reading so that you can build up a complete picture as you go through the book. Chapter One tells you all about your animal sign and the characteristics that are associated with it, while Chapter Two reveals your compatibility with the other animal signs of Chinese astrology. In Chapter Three you can find out more about the sixty-year cycle and the fortune associated with your particular type of animal (there are five different variations of each animal sign). In Chapter Four you can discover the readings related to your Chinese hour, day and month of birth. Finally, Chapter Five introduces you to the lesser-known "Three Lives" system, which enables you to draw up a wide range of personal

readings using a number of different methods, including stars, gods, bones and creatures.

All the horoscope readings exert their own influence over different aspects of your life, and reveal characteristics, personality traits, skills and forecasts associated with your date of birth. However, do remember that although the readings reveal your fortune according to Chinese astrology, it is up to you how you interpret the information. According to Chinese divination, you are born within certain parameters: your family circumstances and personality traits may have been determined but the fate that lies ahead of you has not been fixed. You continue to shape your fortune through the actions you take during your lifetime, and thus the final version of your life ultimately remains in your hands.

Rat

1936 Jan 24 to Feb 10 **1937**
1948 Feb 10 to Jan 28 **1949**
1960 Jan 28 to Feb 14 **1961**
1972 Feb 15 to Feb 2 **1973**
1984 Feb 2 to Feb 19 **1985**
1996 Feb 19 to Feb 6 **1997**
2008 Feb 7 to Jan 25 **2009**
2020 Jan 25 to Feb 11 **2021**

Dragon

1940 Feb 8 to Jan 26 **1941**
1952 Jan 27 to Feb 13 **1953**
1964 Feb 13 to Feb 1 **1965**
1976 Jan 31 to Feb 17 **1977**
1988 Feb 17 to Feb 5 **1989**
2000 Feb 5 to Jan 23 **2001**
2012 Jan 23 to Feb 9 **2013**
2024 Feb 10 to Jan 28 **2025**

Monkey

1944 Jan 25 to Feb 12 **1945**
1956 Feb 12 to Jan 30 **1957**
1968 Jan 30 to Feb 16 **1969**
1980 Feb 16 to Feb 4 **1981**
1992 Feb 4 to Jan 22 **1993**
2004 Jan 22 to Feb 8 **2005**
2016 Feb 8 to Jan 27 **2017**
2028 Jan 26 to Feb 12 **2029**

Ox

1937 Feb 11 to Jan 30 **1938**
1949 Jan 29 to Feb 16 **1950**
1961 Feb 15 to Feb 4 **1962**
1973 Feb 3 to Jan 22 **1974**
1985 Feb 20 to Feb 8 **1986**
1997 Feb 7 to Jan 27 **1998**
2009 Jan 26 to Feb 13 **2010**
2021 Feb 12 to Jan 31 **2022**

Snake

1941 Jan 27 to Feb 14 **1942**
1953 Feb 14 to Feb 2 **1954**
1965 Feb 2 to Jan 20 **1966**
1977 Feb 18 to Feb 6 **1978**
1989 Feb 6 to Jan 26 **1990**
2001 Jan 24 to Feb 11 **2002**
2013 Feb 10 to Jan 30 **2014**
2025 Jan 29 to Feb 16 **2026**

Rooster

1945 Feb 13 to Feb 1 **1946**
1957 Jan 31 to Feb 17 **1958**
1969 Feb 17 to Feb 5 **1970**
1981 Feb 5 to Jan 24 **1982**
1993 Jan 23 to Feb 9 **1994**
2005 Feb 9 to Jan 28 **2006**
2017 Jan 28 to Feb 15 **2018**
2029 Feb 13 to Feb 2 **2030**

Tiger

1938 Jan 31 to Feb 18 **1939**
1950 Feb 17 to Feb 5 **1951**
1962 Feb 5 to Jan 24 **1963**
1974 Jan 23 to Feb 10 **1975**
1986 Feb 9 to Jan 28 **1987**
1998 Jan 28 to Feb 15 **1999**
2010 Feb 14 to Feb 2 **2011**
2022 Feb 1 to Jan 21 **2023**

Horse

1942 Feb 15 to Feb 4 **1943**
1954 Feb 3 to Jan 23 **1955**
1966 Jan 21 to Feb 8 **1962**
1978 Feb 7 to Jan 27 **1979**
1990 Jan 27 to Feb 14 **1991**
2002 Feb 12 to Jan 31 **2003**
2014 Jan 31 to Feb 18 **2015**
2026 Feb 17 to Feb 5 **2027**

Dog

1946 Feb 2 to Jan 21 **1947**
1958 Feb 18 to Feb 7 **1959**
1970 Feb 6 to Jan 26 **1971**
1982 Jan 25 to Feb 12 **1983**
1994 Feb 10 to Jan 30 **1995**
2006 Jan 29 to Feb 17 **2007**
2018 Feb 16 to Feb 4 **2019**
2030 Feb 3 to Jan 22 **2031**

Rabbit

1939 Feb 19 to Feb 7 **1940**
1951 Feb 6 to Jan 26 **1952**
1963 Jan 25 to Feb 12 **1964**
1975 Feb 11 to Jan 30 **1976**
1987 Jan 29 to Feb 16 **1988**
1999 Feb 16 to Feb 4 **2000**
2011 Feb 3 to Jan 22 **2012**
2023 Jan 22 to Feb 9 **2024**

Ram

1943 Feb 5 to Jan 24 **1944**
1955 Jan 24 to Feb 11 **1956**
1967 Feb 9 to Jan 29 **1968**
1979 Jan 28 to Feb 15 **1980**
1991 Feb 15 to Feb 3 **1992**
2003 Feb 1 to Jan 21 **2004**
2015 Feb 19 to Feb 7 **2016**
2027 Feb 6 to Jan 25 **2028**

Pig

1947 Jan 22 to Feb 9 **1948**
1959 Feb 8 to Jan 27 **1960**
1971 Jan 27 to Feb 14 **1972**
1983 Feb 13 to Feb 1 **1984**
1995 Jan 31 to Feb 18 **1996**
2007 Feb 18 to Feb 6 **2008**
2019 Feb 5 to Jan 24 **2020**
2031 Jan 23 to Feb 10 **2032**

The twelve
ANIMAL SIGNS

On the first day of the Chinese new year, one of the twelve animals takes its place for the year. The animal years work in a continuous cycle, beginning with the rat and ending with the pig. Each animal rules once every twelve years and has its own particular characteristics that influence the nature of your life.

There are numerous Chinese myths surrounding the twelve animals. Included in this chapter are traditional stories of how each animal gained a place as one of the twelve signs chosen by the Jade Emperor.

You will also discover just what kind of personality, interests and moods belong to your animal, how to deal with relationships on both a personal and professional level, and even to which occupations you are most suited.

The Chinese calendar follows the cycles of the moon, and the Chinese year always begins slightly later than the Western year. You can find out your animal sign by referring to the dates listed on the page opposite; check the date on which the year begins – if you were born in January or February you may belong to the previous animal year.

Rat

When the Jade Emperor first chose the animal signs, he worked out two basic criteria. Any animal that wanted to be accepted either had to be of use to humanity or be one of the first to arrive at the Heavenly Palace on the day when the animals were being chosen.

The rat desperately wanted to get in but realized he was of little use to humanity, so he decided to use his cunning to get into the palace first. He knew the ox was noted for reliability and would probably be the first to arrive, so, early in the morning on the allocated day, he jumped onto the ox's horn.

The ox was indeed the first to arrive at the palace – so early that the doors of the palace were still closed. The ox waited expectantly outside while the gates were slowly opened, then suddenly the rat jumped off and ran between the gates. The ox was furious at being cheated; he had made the effort to arrive early and so complained to the Jade Emperor. The Emperor listened but felt that he could not go against his own word, and consequently the cunning rat became the first animal sign.

PERSONALITY

You are active and intelligent, quick to spot the potential in a situation and skilled at putting your ideas into effect. In unexpected situations you are able to quickly assess both the drawbacks and the possibilities, and while others are wondering what to do you have already taken advantage of the opportunity that lies there. You can be strong-willed and ambitious but be careful not to force your ideas on others; a little consideration will prevent you irritating or alienating friends and colleagues.

In your determination to see projects up and running, you can appear to be selfish or stubborn, but you believe in what you are doing and approach it whole-heartedly. You are a good and meticulous organizer and like to be familiar with all the available options should an unexpected difficulty arise. You are

fair in your dealings and expect the same from others in return, and can be deeply affronted if you feel you have been deceived or your trust has been abused. Sometimes you set your targets too high, whether in relationship to your friends or in your career, but as the years pass you will become more realistic and tolerant.

You can be open and gregarious in company and are a welcome addition to a party. You are intelligent in conversation, can detect the humor in a situation and are generous with both your compliments and your attention. But if you find yourself in a situation where you feel that you are not being appreciated, a more petty or critical side may emerge. It is important for you to feel secure and you react anxiously when your position is threatened. You want and need to be understood, but others would be wise not to push or corner you, since those born in the Year of the Rat jealously guard their privacy.

LOVE

You are a passionate and attentive partner and are not afraid of revealing the depths of your feelings. You are full of highly charged emotions, particularly at the start of a relationship. But if you feel your commitment is not returned, resentment will soon creep in. You need to be completely involved and cared for – you want to be part of your partner's plans and also share their thoughts. You are easily hurt if you feel your partner has left you out in the cold, and in response you can be petty and difficult to handle.

   You are likely to pass through many highs and lows in your relationships, which does make them rather fragile. What you need is security, and once you have been reassured, you are attentive and loving. In fact, you can be great company and love to indulge in life's pleasures, but you do not like being reprimanded. You know how to charm, and though romantic game-playing is not your strong point, you also know how to deal with it. It will take time, but when you find someone who gives you the security and love you need, you will be a faithful partner.

CAREER

You are energetic and versatile and can usually find your way around obstacles. You are able to adapt to various environments; it is not unusual for someone born in the Year of the Rat to be involved in several projects besides their main career. You are attentive to your work, and when you are negotiating terms or handling people you can be clever and discriminating, although others may distrust your motives. You are a good tactician, but try to keep colleagues informed in order to maintain their trust.

   If you feel your colleagues are not performing to the standard you expect or are not sharing information, you can be overcritical when more patience or understanding might well resolve the situation. Although you are suited to careers involving buying or selling you are advised to concentrate on small-scale projects.

   You are suited to a career in sales, accountancy or shopkeeping. You would also make a good publisher, writer, musician or outdoor pursuits instructor.

RAT ASSOCIATIONS

 ### Element

WATER In Chinese philosophy the five elements are types of energy that affect all life. It is their interaction that creates change from a global level to a personal level. The rat is associated with the element of water, which works in harmony with the element of wood but is overwhelmed by the element of earth.

 ### Color

BLACK The rat is linked to the color black, which is traditionally associated with honor and dignity. It can reflect honor towards either family, colleagues or country. Black also represents success in the face of difficulty, and it was the color worn by the first emperor of China after he defeated the Chou dynasty.

 ### Yin/Yang

YIN Yin and yang are the two great cosmic forces that influence and balance all life. Yin is cool, watery and still, a force that becomes stronger as summer wanes and the winter season begins. Although the rat embodies both yin and yang qualities, it is associated with water, which has powerful yin qualities linked to peace and reflection.

 ### Direction

NORTH Each of the twelve animal signs is matched to a direction of the compass. The rat is linked to a northerly direction, which in turn is associated with the late hours of the day and first hours of the morning. The north is traditionally linked to midwinter, a time when yin is at its strongest.

The ox was one of the first servants of the Heavenly Palace, often acting as a messenger between heaven and earth. One year, the land was bleak and the herders begged the Jade Emperor to send new grass to feed their animals. The ox eagerly volunteered for the job and was instructed to sow a handful of seeds every three steps.

He set forth happily, but he was so pleased with himself that he stumbled over the gates of the palace and fell to earth unconscious, scattering the seeds everywhere. The following year, all the land was covered with grass and no grain could be planted. Angry, the Jade Emperor summoned the ox to him. The ox confessed meekly and the Emperor ordered him to eat the grass and help the farmers himself. He was then bodily hauled out of heaven and landed on earth with a crack, knocking his upper teeth, which is why oxen today have peculiar front teeth.

The ox was a dedicated worker and keen to seek forgiveness, so he paid his debt to humanity ten times over. When the signs were being chosen, the farmers cheerfully recommended the animal that had once ruined their crops, and the Jade Emperor duly gave him a place among the twelve animal signs.

PERSONALITY

You have a quiet and steady nature and are perseverant, even in the most trying circumstances, because once you have made a commitment you keep your word. You need peace and quiet to work through your ideas, and when you have set your mind on something it is hard for you to be convinced otherwise. Your plans and ideas are built on firm ground – you are unlikely to be swept off your feet by fascinating but unrealistic schemes – and your logical approach often pays off in the long term. You are measured in your judgements and are wary of excitable or unpredictable behavior, although sometimes you are so set in your opinions that it prejudices your actions. Underneath your calm exterior, you can be as stubborn and hot-headed as an ox if pushed against your will or forced to change your position. You then need to be left alone to regain your composure, and others are advised to keep clear during this cooling-off period.

You are not extravagant, and the thought of living off credit cards or being in debt makes you nervous – indeed, the possibility of taking a serious risk could cause you many sleepless nights. You are truthful and sincere, and the idea of wheeling and dealing in a competitive world is distasteful to you – in fact, people born in the ox years are rarely driven by the prospect of financial gain. You are well-liked because of your honesty and patience, and your close friends appreciate the fact that you are rather introverted and wary of new trends, although every now and then you can be encouraged to try something new. When secure in your environment, you are sociable and relaxed, but occasionally a dark cloud looms over you and you take on the worries of the world, mulling over the problems you see and trying to find solutions.

LOVE

You are gentle and open with the right partner, and will thrive on strong love and support. But, in the search for a compatible relationship, you have to tread cautiously, since you are easily hurt. Not driven by romance, you have to be persuaded to accept invitations, to experiment with your appearance and to be more adventurous in general.

Your ideal partner is truthful and gentle but knows how to cajole and tease you. Although there may be times when you misinterpret light-hearted remarks or fail to see the humor in a situation, with a little encouragement and reassurance you will find that you are able to throw off your worries and you can begin to enjoy yourself. Your ideal partner also has the enthusiasm to introduce you to new interests but, at the same time, will not take risks that threaten your security. You can tolerate weaknesses in your partner, and when there are emotional upheavals you will consider whether the blame lies with you; however, if you have been deceived you find it hard to forgive.

CAREER

If you feel that projects are being finalized or decisions made with insufficient attention to detail, it will not be long before you express your concern. You approach work seriously, and as long as you are not forced into the public eye you are able to think clearly and plan meticulously. Your reactions may be a little on the slow side, but you are a skilled organizer and logical thinker, and, as the years pass, your determination is likely to be rewarded.

You are able to accept authority and are comfortable in a working environment as long as you know that the business is established on firm foundations. You prefer to know your schedule or timetable, and although you can rise to challenges and, to some extent, deal with the unpredictable, you would rather be well-informed and work within a fixed framework.

You are suited to a career in farming, gardening, estate management, medicine or religion. You would also make a good philosopher, teacher, chef or member of the police force.

OX ASSOCIATIONS

Element

EARTH In Chinese philosophy the five elements are types of energy that affect all life. It is their interaction that creates change from a global level to a personal level. The ox is associated with the element of earth, which works in harmony with the element of metal but is overwhelmed by the element of wood.

Color

YELLOW The ox is linked to the color yellow, which was the imperial color of China – the color reserved for the emperor. Yellow is associated with progress, fame and achievement. It is also linked to the element of earth since the fertile soils in many areas of China have a yellow hue.

Yin/Yang

YIN AND YANG Yin and yang are the two great cosmic forces that influence and balance all life. Yin is cool, watery and still while yang is hot, heavy and dynamic. The ox is associated with the element of earth, in which yin and yang are equally balanced, a combination that is linked to thought and care.

Direction

NORTH-NORTH-EAST Each of the twelve animal signs is matched to a direction of the compass. The ox is linked to a north-north-easterly direction, which in turn is associated with the very early hours of the morning. This direction is also traditionally linked to the end of winter, a time when yin still has strength but yang is beginning to grow.

Tiger

Originally the tiger was an ordinary and harmless animal. It was through his own dedication and toughness that he became the fearsome animal that he is today, learning the arts of pouncing, clutching and biting from his teacher, the cat. Consequently, the Jade Emperor made him the guard of heaven.

Shortly after the tiger became guard, the animals on earth began to hunt and eat humans. The people pleaded for protection, and the Emperor sent the tiger to control the other animals. The tiger fought many great battles with the lion, horse and bear, and before long the other animals were behaving themselves. Soon afterwards, the great turtle of the sea began causing the sea to flood human lands, so the tiger defeated him in battle and slew him. As a reward, the Emperor marked the tiger's skin with one stroke for every animal he had defeated and made him king of all animals.

After causing disturbances on earth, the lion – originally a member of the twelve animal signs – was stripped of his place. The tiger was immediately appointed his kingly successor and became one of the most prominent and powerful signs.

PERSONALITY

You enjoy life and are excited by new challenges, unusual places and unexpected events. Your positive attitude is attractive to others, and your enthusiasm and will to succeed easily draw a following. Your determination is not always enough to see you through, and you do not like to lose face or be seen to fail; more than likely you will find a new challenge and start over again.

Your attention is caught by the unpredictable, and while others may be cautious, you are not afraid to explore the potential in unlikely situations. Simply being told that something is exciting is usually not sufficient for you – what you really need is first-hand experience. You have a generous nature and involve friends in your plans, but if threatened you are likely to withdraw and you can be aggressive when trapped.

As soon as you have regained your sense of security, your confidence also returns, enabling you to set out on your adventures once more.

You trust your instincts and usually follow them, although there is a more objective side to your nature, which assesses situations thoughtfully. Occasionally you will be hurt along the way by putting your trust too firmly in the wrong person, yet at other times you can be too critical or suspicious. If you have been disappointed or disillusioned, you eventually pick yourself up, dust yourself down and head off on a new road.

While your friends admire your optimism, at times they may find it hard to share your enthusiasm, and those who cannot challenge or charm may be pushed to one side. You are an exciting, courageous and generous friend, but if you do not achieve what you want you can also be obstinate and self-centered. Inevitably, there will be highs and lows in your friendships, but deep down your loyalty remains firm.

LOVE

Your enthusiasm for life spills over into your relationships, and it is not unusual for you to flit from one partnership into another, inspired by each one. You are excited by the possibilities that each relationship presents and are carried along by the first rush of romance. But, eventually, when boredom or predictability sets in, you will be off in search of a new partner. Even when romance collapses around you, you may be feeling low for a while, but you will soon regain energy in pursuit of a new partnership.

People with an independent character attract you: although they may be stimulated by your company and admire your energy, they can still manage without you. A relationship with someone who shares your sense of adventure but still pursues their own interests is more likely to succeed. You are not afraid to declare your feelings and are honest with your emotions, but you are also changeable. You need a partner who remains steady and constant, and quietly pursues their own plans.

CAREER

Optimism, determination and initiative are your strong points. You can be inspired by people or places, a chance remark or something you have unexpectedly seen, and then you head off with an infectious enthusiasm. Some of these projects will succeed because you have the drive to see them through to the end, and you are an efficient and stimulating leader. You do not, however, deal well with failure and are embarrassed when colleagues discover that you have misjudged situations.

When you are making plans, you are not sidetracked by the trivial and usually avoid elaborate arrangements – you prefer tackling the job directly rather than creating an unnecessary fuss. Your ability to cut through the side issues, and your energetic response to challenges, will serve you well in your career. The appeal of work for you is generally in the excitement and the quality, not the profit.

You are suited to a career in travel, design or politics. You would also make a good soldier, police officer, travel writer, explorer and advertising or business executive.

TIGER ASSOCIATIONS

Element

WOOD In Chinese philosophy the five elements are types of energy that affect all life. It is their interaction that creates change from a global level to a personal level. The tiger is associated with the element of wood, which works in harmony with the element of fire but is overwhelmed by the element of metal.

Color

GREEN The tiger is linked to the color green, which is associated with the season of spring. It is the color of new life, tranquillity and relaxation. It is said that dreams will end well if they feature the color green, since it is a lucky and influential color, particularly when combined with the color red.

Yin/Yang

YANG Yin and yang are the two great cosmic forces that influence and balance all life. Yang is hot, heavy and dynamic, a force which becomes stronger as winter wanes and the summer begins. Although the tiger embodies both yin and yang qualities, it is associated with wood, which has powerful yang qualities linked to relaxation and intuition.

Direction

EAST-NORTH-EAST Each of the twelve animal signs is matched to a direction of the compass. The tiger is linked to an east-north-easterly direction, which in turn is associated with the hours leading up to dawn. This direction is also traditionally linked to the beginning of spring, as yang begins its ascendancy and yin begins to weaken.

Rabbit

In ancient times the rabbit and the ox were friendly neighbors, but one day they fell into an argument. The rabbit maintained that he was the champion runner of all the animals and that the ox could never equal him because the ox lacked his light body. Insulted, the ox began to train every day, determined to beat the rabbit.

When the time came for the animal signs to be chosen, all the animals wanted to be first at the palace in order to get a place. The ox and the rabbit decided to run together, but the rabbit broke his promise. Rising early, he dashed off at a great pace and, after a while, turned round to look for the other animals. To his delight, not one was in sight, so he settled down for a nap, confident that he would be the first.

The rabbit woke up suddenly to find the tiger overtaking him. Panicking, he sprinted as fast as he could to the palace, arriving to find that both the tiger and the ox had run faster than him, and that the rat had snatched first place through his cunning. Consequently, he was only fourth! Bitter at the ox, he moved his home underground, where his descendants still dwell today.

PERSONALITY

You have a tranquil nature and are sensitive to the world around you. You cannot thrive in a competitive or aggressive environment, and you soon become anxious if you are forced to take risks. Your delicately balanced emotions are easily destabilized by unsettled or unpredictable situations, and you instinctively want to create a peaceful and comfortable atmosphere. In fact, this makes you a very hospitable host, attentive to the needs of others, ensuring that they do not feel isolated or neglected. You are aware that small details are important in creating the right ambience and you pay attention to everything, from color, design and furniture to food and conversation. When you are certain that everything is arranged to your satisfaction you can then relax – and you make charming, elegant and intelligent company.

You have a good imagination and intellect, combined with an openness and a generosity that enable you to turn enemies into friends. Your approach to life is not threatening or disruptive, and the only time that you are really obstinate is when you feel you have been pushed beyond your capabilities. When faced with a dilemma, or if you are just feeling low, you tend to keep your thoughts well hidden in the belief that it is not appropriate for you to make demands or force your opinions on others.

Your lifestyle is conservative as you do not like your security compromised, but when you opt for safety over risk you may miss good opportunities. You have no desire to be in the limelight; you shy away from confrontations or complications, and if there is an escape route you will quickly take it.

This does not imply that you are frivolous or irresponsible, for when you truly believe in something you are serious, perseverant and capable.

LOVE

You need trust, security and tenderness in a relationship, and are happiest when you can create an intimate and cosy atmosphere. You are unlikely to go in search of emotional thrills and do not thrive on romantic upheavals, so when a partner's behavior becomes erratic or hurtful you withdraw into your shell. There are times when you are confident in love, but an unpredictable action or careless remark can suddenly place serious doubts in your mind. Try to express your concerns and you may well find that your doubts are groundless. When you have found the right partner, the affection that you offer will be returned, and you will prove to be both sympathetic and forgiving, far more likely to listen to someone else's problems than to reveal your own.

You are happy sharing artistic interests, informal dinners and stimulating conversation. It will take time to find the soulmate you are searching for and along the way you may appear fickle, but when you have found that person your commitment is powerful.

CAREER

Your intelligence and imagination stand you in good stead in your career, and you always give careful thought to projects before you undertake them. You are balanced in outlook and cautious in approach, and you like to be informed of all the facts before you make a judgement. You do not enjoy the cut and thrust of business life, preferring work that is more methodical and reliable, and thus the worlds of politics and finance hold little interest for you. Working under pressure makes you nervous, as do sudden demands on you to develop creative ideas, and while others may thrive on heated discussion you prefer reasoned debate. Your creative talents will come to the fore when you are allowed to work at your own pace. Many colleagues appreciate your tact and modesty and realize you are a conscientious worker, unlikely to step over others to achieve your goals.

You are suited to a career in literature, art, design or public relations. You would also be a good counsellor, barrister, judge, solicitor, adviser or secretary.

RABBIT ASSOCIATIONS

Element

WOOD In Chinese philosophy the five elements are types of energy that affect all life. It is their interaction that creates change from a global level to a personal level. The rabbit is associated with the element of wood, which works in harmony with the element of fire but is overwhelmed by the element of metal.

Color

GREEN The rabbit is linked to the color green, which is associated with the season of spring. It is the color of new life, tranquillity and relaxation. It is said that dreams will end well if they feature the color green since it is a lucky and influential color, particularly when combined with the color red.

Yin/Yang

YIN AND YANG Yin and yang are the two great cosmic forces that influence and balance all life. Yin is cool, watery and still, while yang is hot, heavy and dynamic. The rabbit is associated with the element of earth, in which yin and yang are equally balanced – a combination that is linked to thought and care.

Direction

EAST Each of the twelve animal signs is matched to a direction of the compass. The rabbit is linked to an easterly direction, which in turn is associated with the hours of sunrise. This direction is also traditionally linked to the middle of spring, a time when yang continues to gain influence as yin declines.

Dragon

The dragon was an ambitious animal, and wanted to take the tiger's place as king of the animals. Consequently, fighting broke out between the two, but neither had a clear advantage. The Jade Emperor decided to judge between them.

When the dragon heard this news he became worried that he did not look impressive enough. At this time, the dragon did not have a horn – it was, in fact, the rooster who could boast this possession – and so the centipede suggested that the dragon borrow the rooster's horn. Although the rooster refused at first, the centipede offered to guarantee the dragon's honesty, and the rooster, the centipede's friend, then agreed to the request.

When the dragon and the tiger came to be judged, both looked awesome and ferocious. The Emperor decided to make the dragon king of the water and the tiger king of the earth. As the tiger was already an animal sign, the dragon was given the same status. However, the dragon was reluctant to return the horn and kept it as a symbol of his status. Angered, the rooster went after the centipede, who hid underground. To this day, roosters love to eat centipedes, and the noise they make is actually their loud cursing about the dragon's theft all those years ago.

PERSONALITY

You have a natural charisma and it is unlikely that you would fade into the background or escape unnoticed at a party. You are lively company, interested in the world around you and excited by new possibilities. You have great energy and self-confidence and know how to create an impression. Many dragon people are exhibitionists, full of energy and enthusiasm; they are also proud, which is sometimes interpreted by onlookers as arrogance. It is true that you are sure of yourself and enjoy being the center of attention, but you also have a brave and charitable side to your character. If a friend is faced by a problem or dilemma you will be there to offer help, and when others might withdraw you will step forwards to help resolve the situation with authority and dignity. In fact, you apply yourself wholeheartedly to most situations, and if you become frustrated with others it is only because they do not have your stamina or skills. You demand high standards of yourself and are surprised when others cannot keep up with you; in your drive to complete the task you fail to see their weaknesses.

The Chinese say that heaven and earth are balanced in the life of someone born in this year, and success certainly seems to follow you. You are decisive and frank, capable and also lucky. As well as being blessed with good fortune, you are also an able judge of situations, stepping in at the right moment with an exciting or creative scheme. You can be quick-tempered and obstinate, and sometimes too outspoken, but there is usually good advice in your criticisms or suggestions. You believe that you are acting with good intentions and are confident of a positive outcome, and more often than not events work out as you had hoped.

LOVE

You have an impressive presence and it is not unusual for you to have a string of admirers who are drawn by your charisma. You are attractive and know how to charm, so before long your partner will be under your spell. It is easy for you to find romance but hard for you to settle down – numerous love affairs are not uncommon for those born in the Year of the Dragon. You do not set out to conquer someone romantically and then leave them for a new challenge; it is just that you are disappointed when you uncover weaknesses. You are frustrated by emotional overdependence or indecision, and will eventually set off in search of a new and exciting romance.

At one level, love is a game, and you rarely yearn for the past or harbor regrets. The same cannot be said for your ex-lovers, who may carry a torch for you long after the romance is over. You need someone who gives you the space to express yourself – to impress and to perform – someone who plays an active role but yet is not threatened by your exuberance.

CAREER

You enjoy positions of responsibility and your presence does command attention. You know how to gain respect, and being in charge or giving orders comes naturally; fortunately, most people accept your authority. It is important for you to have new challenges and freedom of movement; when you feel trapped by your career or at the mercy of other people's decisions you are likely to pack your bags and leave.

You are an able and intelligent worker and have strong opinions on the planning and execution of projects. If there is room for doubt, hold back, seek advice or wait until you are certain that the conditions are right. You have good leadership qualities and are usually fair in your dealings, but your energy can be overwhelming. In your planning you have to allow for the fact that some colleagues cannot match your pace, even though they may be inspired by your ideas.

You are suited to a career in law, religion or the arts. You would also be a good manager, entrepreneur, doctor or actor.

DRAGON ASSOCIATIONS

 ## Element

EARTH In Chinese philosophy the five elements are types of energy that affect all life. It is their interaction that creates change from a global level to a personal level. The dragon is associated with the element of earth, which works in harmony with the element of metal but is overwhelmed by the element of wood.

 ## Color

YELLOW The dragon is linked to the color yellow, which was the imperial color of China – the color reserved for the emperor. Yellow is associated with progress, fame and achievement. It is also linked to the element of earth since the fertile soils in many areas of China have a yellow hue.

 ## Yin/Yang

YIN AND YANG Yin and yang are the two great cosmic forces that influence and balance all life. Yin is cool, watery and still, while yang is hot, heavy and dynamic. The dragon is associated with the element of earth, in which yin and yang are equally balanced, a combination that is linked to thought and care.

 ## Direction

EAST-SOUTH-EAST Each of the twelve animal signs is matched to a direction of the compass. The dragon is linked to an east-south-easterly direction, which in turn is associated with the early hours of the day as the sun is beginning to climb. This direction is also linked to the end of spring, as yang gains increasing strength.

Snake

A long time ago, the snake and the frog were very good friends. Then, however, the snake had four legs and the frog had none, crawling on his belly as the snake does today. Ironically, the snake was lazy and relied on the frog to catch insects for him; in doing this, the frog also helped the people by getting rid of pests, so naturally the people liked the frog and distrusted the snake.

Angered by this, the snake began to bite humans and their animals, hurting – even killing – many people. Although the snake was summoned before the Jade Emperor and asked to stop, he was an obstinate animal and he continued. As a punishment, his four legs were taken from him and given to the frog.

Ashamed by his past behavior, the snake turned his efforts towards helping the people, in an attempt to redeem himself. He helped his relative the dragon to control the rains and he donated his body to be made into medicine after his death. Impressed, the Emperor gave the snake a place just after the dragon in the animal signs. Although this pleased the snake, he could not help hating the frog for stealing his legs – which is why snakes still try to eat frogs today.

PERSONALITY

You are decisive and active, stimulated by thoughtful debate and interesting conversation, although if the conversation becomes repetitive your attention soon wanders. It is unlikely that you will tolerate idle chatter for long, preferring instead to focus on new ideas and intelligent discussion. When you find a particular topic stimulating, you often make unusual and challenging contributions.

You are a good judge of situations and are alert to new possibilities, so when you have an idea you pursue it persistently and energetically. You are often so confident of its success that you fail to listen to constructive advice, but what really disturbs you is the thought of actually being proved wrong. Although you do not easily take advice, you are

patient with others when they need your help, and your ability to look at a problem from a variety of angles is appreciated. When faced with a dilemma, you are cool and reserved, and it is this clarity of vision that enables you to act decisively. You act with speed and conviction when you are committed to a task, since you believe intensely in what you are doing and rarely waste time or energy on projects lacking in good potential.

However, your life is not all work and competition, and when the opportunity arises you know how to wind down and relax. You can only keep up your energetic approach for so long before you find a means of escape and withdraw into a more private world to pursue your hobbies and enjoy life's luxuries. You make trusting and long-term friendships and are a protective and caring friend. Your anger, however, can be quickly aroused, and you will soon retaliate if you think someone has taken advantage of your trust or has hurt those close to you.

LOVE

You have a very seductive nature, and when you have resolved to woo someone you plan your moves carefully and do not abandon your quest lightly. You are a humorous and romantic partner who jealously guards important relationships; even if you wander off to flirt with others, you are determined not to lose what you already have. You like the attention and affection that romance offers but do not want to feel trapped, and you also enjoy discovering new friendships, although this may create tensions for the partner left behind.

Sometimes you have one set of rules for yourself and one for your partner – you need space to travel and explore without having to account for your movements, yet you keep a wary eye on your partner's activities. But when you are romantically involved, you are also loving and attentive, stimulating and playful, although it takes time for you to reveal your fears or discuss your weaknesses. Ideally you want a partner to give you freedom, but you also like the security of sharing intimate moments in relaxed and cosy surroundings.

CAREER

You can read complex situations quickly and then set about resolving them in a quiet, controlled manner. You enjoy working independently since it gives you the freedom to travel and negotiate on your own terms, as well as allowing you to avoid the possibility of your ideas being limited or even taken over by others. You are a logical and organized worker and have the patience needed to acquire new skills. Many people born in the Year of the Snake are also gifted with a good memory that enables them to carry out projects thoroughly.

You are courageous and determined, able to spot potential trouble and react immediately, but once you have achieved your goal you usually withdraw to gather your thoughts and rest. After relaxing and recuperating, you gather your energies once again to prepare for new challenges.

You are suited to a job in public relations, politics, law or catering. You would also make a good astrologer, archaeologist, entrepreneur, psychologist or philosopher.

SNAKE ASSOCIATIONS

 ## Element

FIRE In Chinese philosophy the five elements are types of energy that affect all life. It is their interaction that creates change from a global level to a personal level. The snake is associated with the element of fire, which works in harmony with the element of earth but is overwhelmed by the element of water.

 ## Color

RED The snake is linked to the color red, which is traditionally associated with good fortune. It is linked to happiness and strength, success in projects and prosperity in the family. It is one of the most popular colors at Chinese new year, when blessings are written on red paper and attached to doors or gates.

 ## Yin/Yang

YANG Yin and yang are the two great cosmic forces that influence and balance all life. Yang is hot, heavy and dynamic, a force that becomes stronger as winter wanes and the summer begins. Although the snake embodies both yin and yang qualities, it is associated with wood, which has powerful yang qualities linked to relaxation and intuition.

 ## Direction

SOUTH-SOUTH-EAST Each of the twelve animal signs is matched to a direction of the compass. The snake is linked to a south-south-easterly direction, which in turn is associated with the late hours of the morning, as the sun is climbing high in the sky. This direction is also linked to the early summer, when yang is approaching its peak.

Horse

When the horse first served the Jade Emperor in heaven, he had a magnificent pair of wings. He could soar around the sky, swim in the sea and run on the earth. Arrogant and haughty, he bullied the other animals.

One day he was asked to take a message to the Dragon King of the East Sea. Stopped by the King's guards on his way into the palace, he became furious and kicked an unfortunate guard to death. When the Emperor heard of this, he ordered that the horse's wings be cut off and the horse placed underneath a great mountain.

After two hundred years of agony beneath the mountain, the ancestor of humanity passed by. Hearing him, the horse cried out that he wished to dedicate his life to serving humanity. The ancestor was moved by this and used magic to free the horse. In thanks, the horse dedicated himself to humans, ploughing the fields, transporting goods and fighting bravely in battle. Consequently, when the animal signs were being chosen, the horse was one of the first to be recommended by the people, and was duly appointed by the Jade Emperor in acknowledgement of their wishes.

PERSONALITY

You are independent and confident and usually have a welcoming smile for both old friends and new acquaintances. You thrive in lively company, and as well as being a gregarious companion you are an eloquent and inspiring speaker. You like to be recognized for your skills and are easily flattered, but you also have an honesty and a genuine warmth that attract many friends. People confide in you because you are interested in their thoughts and feelings, but you are so excited by new discoveries that you find it hard to keep a secret. This is not something that arises out of malice or revenge – sometimes you just cannot help yourself. The same could also happen when you take on new interests or projects: in your eagerness to begin or to organize, you may offend others or unknowingly interfere with long-standing plans.

You are inspired by ideas and tend to act on them without delay, carried away by the excitement of the moment, but there is a danger that you are too impulsive and do not give enough thought to the future. When you are disillusioned by the outcome of your efforts, you then turn your attention to a new project and head off once again, brimming with new ideas. The thought of failing and having to pick up the pieces fills you with anxiety, and rather than dealing with this prospect you prefer to change course so that your energies are focused in another direction. Sometimes this drive and excitement serves you well, since it creates many openings and possibilities, but there are times when it leaves plans half-finished. You are always ready to offer good advice and can be very persuasive, but your confident

which makes you a welcome addition to a party, but there is also a deeper, more tender side to your nature, which is moved when you see someone in trouble.

LOVE

You are attracted by romance and its excitement, and you probably have a lively love life. Partners are drawn by your openness, good humor and interest in the world around you. You know how to put people at ease, and even the most shy person could soon be caught up in your enthusiasm for a new scheme. The difficulty lies in making a commitment; but when you finally settle down you rarely stray.

When you begin a relationship, you can occasionally be unpredictable or childish: your partner may make a small mistake and you take it as an insult, or you suddenly have a mood swing for no apparent reason. It will not take long for the right partner to calm this nervousness and insecurity. Once the relationship is established, you prove to be a supportive, adaptable and dependable partner. Your capacity to be charming and your energy and cheerfulness also enable you to create firm friendships. Even when a relationship is over, you will probably still be there if former partners need you in times of trouble.

CAREER

Your versatility and quick reactions make you suitable for a wide variety of jobs. Those born in the Year of the Monkey are intelligent, usually well-read and often intellectual; and once you set yourself a target you rarely fail to achieve it. There are certain skills that you can acquire easily and these are the ones to concentrate on; you should know your limits and not gamble or speculate. In fact, most monkey people are good at assessing risks and have a keen sense of financial situations. You rise to new challenges and hammer away at a problem until you find a solution. Even when a situation looks disheartening, you explore all possible avenues until you find a promising opening. Your good organizational skills, combined with an astute and creative approach, are suited to work that involves investigation and speedy responses.

You are suited to a career in media, finance, management, the police or public relations. You would also be a good designer, skilled manual worker, planner or surveyor.

MONKEY ASSOCIATIONS

 ### Element

METAL In Chinese philosophy the five elements are types of energy that affect all life. It is their interaction that creates change from a global level to a personal level. The monkey is associated with the element of metal, which works in harmony with the element of water but is overwhelmed by the element of fire.

 ### Color

WHITE The monkey is linked to the color white, which is traditionally associated with autumn and maturity. White is also linked with purity, cleanliness and freshness. Although white clothing is worn in China during times of loss, white can also denote good fortune; white birds, particularly, are a sign of good luck.

 ### Yin/Yang

YIN Yin and yang are the two great cosmic forces that influence and balance all life. Yin is cool, watery and still, a force that becomes stronger as summer wanes and the winter season begins. Although the monkey embodies both yin and yang qualities, it is associated with water, which has powerful yin qualities linked to peace and reflection.

 ### Direction

WEST-SOUTH-WEST Each of the twelve animal signs is matched to a direction of the compass. The monkey is linked to a west-south-westerly direction, which in turn is associated with the late afternoon, when the sun is lower in the sky. This direction is also traditionally linked to the early autumn, as yin begins to gain strength.

Rooster

Originally, the rooster was a disruptive and aggressive animal. When the twelve signs were being chosen, he was not considered as a candidate. Disturbed, he spoke to his friend the horse, asking him how he had been chosen.

The horse replied that it was simple – he helped the people by ploughing the land, bearing goods and fighting in wartime. The rooster said that he would also like to be a sign. "You will have to do something for humanity, then," replied the horse. "All the others do – the ox ploughs, the pig provides meat, the dragon controls the rain. You have a wonderful voice; why not use that?"

The rooster thought this over and came to a decision. He began to use his voice to wake people in the morning so that they could get to work. Moved, the people asked the Jade Emperor to grant him a place in the competition. Although flying animals were not allowed to compete, the Emperor made an exception and placed a flower on the rooster's head to show he could take part. During the great race, the dog and the rooster were neck and neck until, as they were nearing the finish, the rooster resorted to flying to arrive before the dog to gain a place as the tenth sign. Since then, the dog has hated the rooster, which is why dogs chase roosters to this day.

PERSONALITY

You enjoy being in the spotlight, entertaining friends and meeting new people, and you can be charming company even in the most unexpected circumstances. It is rare to see you looking dowdy or untidy – in fact, you are usually one of the best dressed and groomed of all the animal signs. You take an active interest in clothes, colors, designs and accessories, and can be just as critical about your own appearance as you are about that of others. You like to keep the conversation flowing and are unlikely to initiate in-depth discussion, although this light-hearted front hides a good intellect. Others may criticize you for being an exhibitionist – and no doubt there are times when you would agree with this – but there is also a compassionate, wise and brave side to your nature, which comes to the fore when others need your help.

You have a strong, independent spirit, which makes it hard for you to accept advice. You are confident in your own judgements and choices, and you prefer to follow your own routine. You can be straightforward to the point of hurting others, and when something needs to be said you go ahead and say it. This directness stems from naivety, not from vindictiveness, since you believe that honesty is the best policy. There are times, though, when, in order to keep the peace, it might be better not to express your opinions.

In many ways you are a good performer, presenting a carefree front, but your real nature is hidden from most people. Your erratic and sometimes even careless

behavior belies a vulnerable streak, and so you tend to protect yourself with humor and lively conversation. Your close friends appreciate your sensitive and courageous side, but acquaintances are only likely to see it in times of crisis.

LOVE

There are likely to be many romantic opportunities in your life since you enjoy courtship and are a charming companion. With your love of good clothes, surroundings and company, you know how to create a romantic atmosphere to suit the moment. You take pride in your appearance, and if the situation demands, you know how to impress with intelligent conversation.

There is a danger that the thrill of romance comes from the conquest, and when a partner's actions or responses become predictable, restlessness takes hold and you set off again in search of a new relationship. Your independent nature keeps you on the move, but you also have a jealous streak, which you try to keep hidden. In the whirl of romance, it is the female rather than the male rooster who usually keeps an eye on practicalities. In the long run, you are a reliable partner, and your roaming will cease when you meet someone you do not want to lose. You are capable of deep commitment, and in the right relationship you are a dedicated and responsible partner.

CAREER

You think clearly and logically but do not like to be put under pressure or pushed to make a decision. If you are allowed to work at a steady pace you are more than capable of achieving a good career. As long as you have the time to think and the freedom to use your imagination, you produce sensible but creative ideas.

If your work is governed by other people, there is a danger that you will feel trapped, which causes you to become overcritical. You are suited to self-employment, and it could be here that your skills are fully recognized and your perseverance rewarded. After working hard to achieve financial security, do not be tempted to spend your earnings quickly or carelessly; this is one of your weak spots, but you can learn to handle your spending with the same steady approach you apply to work.

You are suited to a career in public relations, commercial sales or politics. You would also be a good author, entertainer, beautician or member of the armed forces.

ROOSTER ASSOCIATIONS

 ### Element

METAL In Chinese philosophy the five elements are types of energy that affect all life. It is their interaction that creates change from a global level to a personal level. The rooster is associated with the element of metal, which works in harmony with the element of water but is overwhelmed by the element of fire.

 ### Color

WHITE The rooster is linked to the color white, which is traditionally associated with autumn and maturity. White is also linked with purity, cleanliness and freshness. Although white clothing is worn in China during times of loss, white can also denote good fortune; white birds, particularly, are a sign of good luck.

 ### Yin/Yang

YIN Yin and yang are the two great cosmic forces that influence and balance all life. Yin is cool, watery and still, a force that becomes stronger as summer wanes and the winter season begins. Although the rooster embodies both yin and yang qualities, it is associated with water, which has powerful yin qualities linked to peace and reflection.

 ### Direction

WEST Each of the twelve animal signs is matched to a direction of the compass. The rooster is linked to a westerly direction, which in turn is associated with early evening as the sun begins to set. This direction is also traditionally linked to the middle of autumn, as yin grows increasingly strong.

Dog

When the animal signs were being selected, the cat and the dog were in fierce competition. Each tried to prove that they had done more to help humans. The cat argued that the dog ate too much and all he did was guard the door, while the dog argued that the cat ate all the best food and all he did was scare mice. The argument became so fierce that they turned to the Emperor for judgement.

The Emperor listened, then asked how much food the dog ate every day; the dog replied honestly that he had one bowl of food each meal. When the cat was asked the same question, he lied and claimed that he only had a small bowl of food every meal. Impressed, the Emperor ruled that the cat had a greater claim but that both could take part in the competition.

When the day of the race came, the dog got up early and secured a good place. However, the cat was so scared of the dog attacking him for his lies that he hung behind and came in just after the pig. He thought he was in the first twelve, but the rat had cheated to come first, meaning that the cat had not gained a place as an animal sign. As a result, to this day cats chase rats because they cheated, and, in turn, dogs chase cats because they cheated.

PERSONALITY

You have an honest and courageous nature, ready to fight for a worthy cause or to defend friends in trouble. You are sensitive to others and empathize with them, particularly if they have suffered an injustice, reacting quickly with the same feeling, as though you had been personally offended. Your friends value this trust and loyalty and know that you can be relied upon to keep a promise or remain cool in a crisis. It is rare for you to betray a confidence or withdraw from a commitment.

When you are told a story or hear of an event, you need to know all the facts and are dissatisfied if you feel you have only been given half the story; but, it is precisely this search for the truth that can make you overcritical. You feel it is your duty to point

out weaknesses – not out of spite, but because you feel honesty is the best policy. There are many times, however, when your advice is welcomed and your enthusiasm appreciated. You can inspire confidence without being forceful, and you are not usually misled by appearances or preoccupied with the superfluous.

There is a pessimistic side to your character, and your spirit is drained when you hear of situations beyond your control, such as natural or human disasters. You sometimes find the world overwhelming and need to withdraw from crowds to a quiet place where you can mull over these worries. You want everything to work out in the best possible way and are anxious about the potential problems that may befall you or those around you. Try not to exhaust yourself thinking about problems that have not yet materialized. There is no doubt that you have a strong sense of duty and responsibility, but at times you need to relax and realize that it is impossible to shoulder every burden.

LOVE

You are a good listener and encourage your partner to share their problems, but when it comes to revealing your own feelings you are more reticent, wary of burdening others with your worries. You need reassurance and encouragement, and enjoy the company of someone who has the confident and adventurous spirit that you sometimes lack. You are faithful and tender, but it is important to you that your loyalty is reciprocated. You do not enjoy the excitement of the chase or thrive on jealous scenes, and when you feel isolated you soon become anxious and reserved. It could also take a long time for you to regain your trust once you have been hurt or deceived.

You may find it easier to form a friendship first and let it slowly develop into a romance. But, once committed, you are loving and faithful and will not be slow to defend your partner's reputation. Do not be distressed by imaginings caused by an incidental remark or unintentional criticism when you already know that the relationship is established on firm foundations.

CAREER

You can be relied upon to act responsibly, and can be trusted with sensitive information. You need to have a clear sense of the job description and its final aim, but, once sure of your role, you are a dedicated and steady worker. Avoid aggressive and competitive occupations as these will only make you nervous; focus instead on work that enables you to build trusting relationships with other people.

You are a conscientious colleague, and once you have made a commitment you fulfill it to the best of your ability. Although you can be hesitant – particularly if you are faced by a sudden deadline – you work well as a member of a team and are also an accessible leader. You like to keep the peace with your colleagues, but you are not afraid to stand up in defence of a good cause and will work tirelessly on behalf of others.

You are suited to a career in education, law, social work or research. You would also be a good teacher, doctor, counsellor, campaigner or member of a religious order.

DOG ASSOCIATIONS

 ## Element

EARTH In Chinese philosophy the five elements are types of energy that affect all life. It is their interaction that creates change from a global level to a personal level. The dog is associated with the element of earth, which works in harmony with the element of metal but is overwhelmed by the element of wood.

 ## Color

YELLOW The dog is linked to the color yellow, which was the imperial color of China – the color reserved for the emperor. Yellow is associated with progress, fame and achievement. It is also linked to the element of earth since the fertile soils in many areas of China have a yellow hue.

 ## Yin/Yang

YIN AND YANG Yin and yang are the two great cosmic forces that influence and balance all life. Yin is cool, watery and still, while yang is hot, heavy and dynamic. The dog is associated with the element of earth, in which yin and yang are equally balanced, a combination that is linked to thought and care.

 ## Direction

WEST-NORTH-WEST Each of the twelve animal signs is matched to a direction of the compass. The dog is linked to a west-north-westerly direction, which in turn is associated with the mid-evening hours. This direction is also traditionally linked to the end of autumn, as yin continues to grow strong and yang becomes increasingly weak.

Pig

The pig became an animal sign in a rather unusual way. In ancient times there was a rich senior officer who had no sons. He was desperate to carry on his family line and offered many prayers and sacrifices to the gods. Finally, at the age of sixty, he had a son. In celebration, he held a party and summoned fortune-tellers, who unanimously told him that his son had a promising future.

However, the boy's parents spoiled him and he grew selfish and pampered; and after his father's death he sold off the family fortune to support his lifestyle. Eventually he ran out of money, his friends deserted him and he died in poverty and misery soon afterwards.

Upon arriving in hell after his death, he complained to the Jade Emperor in heaven that he had been unfairly deprived of his promising fate. After further inquiry, the Emperor decided that although the man had been born with a good destiny, he had squandered it. The Emperor punished him by ordering that he be reborn as a pig, "feeding upon the chaff." However, the heavenly officer in charge misheard this as "becoming an animal sign," which sounds very similar in Chinese. As a result, the man was reborn not only as a pig but also as an animal sign.

PERSONALITY

You are well-liked for your honesty and affectionate nature, and when others disappear you are often there to offer support. You are initially reserved with strangers, but as time passes and you gain confidence they discover a lively and warm-hearted disposition. Although your circle of friends and acquaintances is wide, it is only your close friends who share your inner thoughts and feelings. There is an innocence and naivety to your character, combined with an eagerness for new places and experiences. Sometimes this excitability can land you in hot water when you unwittingly say or do something inappropriate, but more often than not you are forgiven since you rarely go out of your way to hurt somebody else. You are not a vengeful person, and if someone has taken advantage of you, you tend to withdraw to reflect on the problem and protect yourself. Given time, you usually find a constructive way to respond.

There is a tolerant and peaceful side to your character, and you allow others their freedom of expression; you do not want to cause an argument any more than be the subject of one. You are not weak, however, and if you have to fight you will rise to the occasion, whether it is to defend yourself or someone else. People think you are a dreamer, and at times you are, but you are also sharp enough to realize what is going on. Your reputation is important to you, and although you are happy to be the target of gentle jokes, you are easily hurt when someone unjustly accuses you or is openly vindictive.

You travel optimistically, hoping to find the best in people – and they sense it. You often find a warm welcome because you are willing to adjust and adapt, and you rarely criticize unless you really feel it is justified.

LOVE

You need to experiment and discover romance before knowing for sure that you have found the right partner. You put your trust in relationships, and some partners take advantage of your apparent naivety. But you are also a good learner and can pick yourself up and start again – it is rare for you ever to feel defeated by a relationship.

Your partner may not realize it, but you are a good observer, making a mental note of what is said or done; though you might appear to be in a dream, you have simply chosen not to comment. You are tolerant and will allow your partner the freedom that you also need, although this has to rest on an affectionate and trustworthy footing. Your lively imagination and enthusiasm soon draw admirers, who share your sense of fun as well as recognize your more sensitive and serious nature. Once a relationship is established, you trust that the love and affection you give will be returned – and it usually is. However, your partner should also be careful not to continually demand your emotional attention, in case you feel trapped.

CAREER

You are not an ambitious person and are quite happy keeping an equilibrium between work and your personal life. Power is not really on your agenda, and it is rare for you to betray a colleague or stab them in the back. You are naturally hard-working and approach tasks seriously and efficiently. In fact, you work well on cooperative projects since they give you a forum to share your ideas.

You like to assess how much work is in front of you and then take it step by step, progressing slowly but surely. Risks make you nervous and you tend to err on the safe side. However, if you do gamble, do not expect to reap huge profits. You are a keen learner, and most pig people are also avid readers, which makes them suited to reflective, studious jobs. But there is also a side to your character that needs human contact, and your patience and kindness are qualities ideal for caring careers.

You are suited to a career in medicine, law or music. You would also make a good writer, researcher, scientist, gardener or landscape artist, librarian or social worker.

PIG ASSOCIATIONS

Element

WATER In Chinese philosophy the five elements are types of energy that affect all life. It is their interaction that creates change from a global level to a personal level. The pig is associated with the element of water, which works in harmony with the element of wood but is overwhelmed by the element of earth.

Color

BLACK The pig is linked to the color black, which is traditionally associated with honor and dignity. It can reflect honor towards family, colleagues or country. Black also represents success in the face of difficulty, and it was the color worn by the first emperor of China after he defeated the Chou dynasty.

Yin/Yang

YIN Yin and yang are the two great cosmic forces that influence and balance all life. Yin is cool, watery and still, a force that becomes stronger as summer wanes and the winter season begins. Although the pig embodies both yin and yang qualities, it is associated with water, which has powerful yin qualities linked to peace and reflection.

Direction

NORTH-NORTH-WEST Each of the twelve animal signs is matched to a direction of the compass. The pig is linked to a north-north-westerly direction, which in turn is associated with the hours of the late evening when the sun has disappeared below the horizon. This direction is also traditionally linked to the early winter, as yin approaches its peak.

2 Animal
COMPATIBILITY

Each of the animal signs has its own strengths and weaknesses. Some are gregarious and passionate, while others are peaceful and reserved; some are easily angered and others quietly perseverant. By now you should be familiar with the characteristics of your own sign, but you may have little idea as to how well you are matched with the other animals.

In this chapter, you will discover just how compatible you are with each of the different animal signs, and also gain useful insight into why you behave the way you do within a relationship. The compatibility readings essentially refer to a romantic partnership, but much of the advice given here can also be applied to relationships between friends or colleagues. For instance, the rat and dragon are compatible at many levels: they are likely to have an exciting romantic relationship but would also be adventurous and intelligent colleagues as well as firm friends. Other signs, however, might require a little more effort to make the relationship work; ways to resolve any differences are suggested in each case.

Interpret the readings according to your situation – and you may well be surprised at just how accurate they are!

FINDING YOUR READING

ANIMAL	Rat	Ox	Tiger	Rabbit	Dragon	Snake	Horse	Ram	Monkey	Rooster	Dog	Pig
Rat	1	2	3	4	5	6	7	8	9	10	11	12
Ox	2	13	14	15	16	17	18	19	20	21	22	23
Tiger	3	14	24	25	26	27	28	29	30	31	32	33
Rabbit	4	15	25	34	35	36	37	38	39	40	41	42
Dragon	5	16	26	35	43	44	45	46	47	48	49	50
Snake	6	17	27	36	44	51	52	53	54	55	56	57
Horse	7	18	28	37	45	52	58	59	60	61	62	63
Ram	8	19	29	38	46	53	59	64	65	66	67	68
Monkey	9	20	30	39	47	54	60	65	69	70	71	72
Rooster	10	21	31	40	48	55	61	66	70	73	74	75
Dog	11	22	32	41	49	56	62	67	71	74	76	77
Pig	12	23	33	42	50	57	63	68	72	75	77	78

Each animal combination corresponds to a number in the grid above. Find your animal sign down the left-hand side of the grid and then find the animal you want to match it with across the top. When you have found both animals, check the number that applies to the pairing and turn to the corresponding reading included on the following pages.

ANIMAL COMBINATIONS

Rat & Rat

You are as intense and passionate as one another, and when you first meet it may seem that the outside world hardly exists as you are so caught up in the pleasure of each other's company. You share a sense of fun and humor, and you are both private and secretive, as well as determined and suspicious. But eventually the highs of this relationship may wear thin simply because you are so similar. If resentment begins to creep in with one partner it will probably also arise in the other, and you will slowly pick at each other's faults. If, however, you realize what is happening and approach this relationship with care, a sense of security can be restored.

Rat & Ox

The ox and the rat appreciate each other's need for independence and privacy, and while the ox is organizing daily affairs, the rat may be devising new schemes or looking for challenging opportunities. Although the rat is astute, the ox can also offer sensible advice, and together they make a determined partnership. There is a natural mutual respect, and when the situation demands, they can both be serious, perseverant workers. There is, however, a side to the rat that is more passionate and gregarious and less controlled than the discreet ox. The rat's sudden lively reactions can sometimes catch the ox unawares, although these unexpected moments usually come as a welcome surprise.

Rat & Tiger

These two signs share a need for stimulation and change, although the rat is not prepared to go as far or as fast as the tiger. The rat enjoys a new challenge and, like the tiger, is often bored by mundane, day-to-day matters. Sometimes, however, the tiger can be too adventurous, which makes the rat feel nervous or isolated. The tiger enjoys romance and flirtation, and in an established relationship the tiger sees this as just having a bit of fun, although it can be rather irritating for the rat. There may also be clashes over the rat's need to feel secure and provided for, in contrast to the tiger's more carefree approach. However, the two signs will be able to find a balance as long as the tiger understands the rat's hopes and fears and tries to make plans and share ideas.

Rat & Dragon

A dragon knows how to charm and captivate a rat, and together they form a lively and adventurous couple. The dragon likes to be the center of attention, winning over an audience and attracting a band of admirers. But the rat is not left in the shadows – sharing in the dragon's plans or games, offering subtle advice and spotting good opportunities. Both signs are gregarious and confident, and are not likely to prevent one another from pursuing their own particular interests. If the rat needs privacy or space, the busy dragon will not object, and when the dragon needs admiration the rat will not be short of compliments.

Rat & Rabbit

The rat's drive and energy may be unnerving for the more peaceful rabbit, and if the rabbit cannot keep up with the pace it might not be long before the rat turns sharp criticism on the hapless rabbit. The rabbit will be able to adapt to a certain extent, but can only deal with a limited amount of unpredictability and mood change. The rat likes a challenge and can be full of passion and determination, but the rabbit may withdraw, unsure of what is going on. The rabbit is the more careful and less competitive of the two signs, although both do share a need for security and comfort in a relationship, and this could be the common ground that allows the relationship to work.

Rat & Snake

You are both astute observers of the world around you, and when a good opportunity appears, you both know how to take advantage of it. There is a certain understanding between you, and sometimes you can read each other's thoughts without a word being spoken. If anything, the rat has more drive than the snake, and when the snake wants to sit back for a well-deserved break the rat may still be negotiating or planning. You can both be lively company, and share a subtle and sharp sense of humor. The rat and the snake are both passionate signs, and although the snake wants fidelity and commitment as much as the rat, this might be harder for the snake to put into practice. The rat may need to give the snake a little more time to commit, and in return the snake will have to learn to be more attentive to this partnership.

Rat & Horse

The emotions of the rat and the horse are likely to run high, and this could initially prove to be a very passionate relationship. For a while the world may pass you by because you are so wrapped up in each other, but before long the rat may pull back. The horse feels the highs and lows of romance very deeply, and, as a result, the realities of work and responsibility take second place. In contrast, the rat keeps a keen eye on what is happening beyond the relationship and will not lose control. The horse's total involvement could irritate the rat, whose sharp criticisms may leave the horse feeling hurt and unfairly treated. For this romance to flourish, the rat has to hold back criticism while the horse calms down to focus of the practicalities of life.

Rat & Monkey

These two signs can find great excitement and energy in each other, but they are both strong characters and there is an element of competition to contend with. If this is kept in check, they can be great company, but it is not unusual for the monkey ultimately to gain the upper hand. In the early stages of a relationship, the monkey may be swept along, but the rat's intensity and passion can be overwhelming, since the monkey does not like to feel out of control. The monkey can be very alluring but is also skilful and could easily emotionally outmanoeuvre the rat. Therefore, the two signs need to establish a balance whereby the rat allows the monkey some space and the monkey, in return, is more emotionally straightforward.

Rat & Ram

The ram finds it hard to keep up with the rat's energy and drive, and would rather be left to take things in their own time. You are both romantics and have a determined streak, but this is expressed in different ways. The rat is good at spotting opportunities and carrying plans through efficiently, while the ram likes to mull life over, taking time out to dream or to create. The rat wants to get going, see a project completed and then be recognized for the skills and effort that they have put in. The ram cannot be pushed in this way, and may well be too preoccupied even to notice the rat's achievements. In order for this partnership to survive and thrive, the ram will have to be more focused and attentive, and the rat more tolerant.

Rat & Rooster

The rat is a good observer and rarely acts on impulse, preferring to analyze situations before making a commitment. The rooster likes to be seen and heard, whereas the resourceful rat chooses their words more skilfully. Initially the rat may only see a superficial side to the rooster's nature and will soon become irritated and critical of their shallowness. The rooster, however, is also courageous and thoughtful. Time and patience is needed to overcome first impressions so that the rat can discover and appreciate the rooster's honesty and openness. The rat, once they really understand the rooster, will find that the two both share a strong critical capacity, and will value the rooster's sharp skills of judgement.

Rat & Dog

The rat and the dog share a need for privacy; the rat guards its independence, while the dog shies away from noise and aggression. In company, the rat is more confident and socially adept, and will give the dog the confidence that may be lacking in public. The dog is often anxious, wondering what problems or pitfalls lie ahead, but the rat keeps a wary eye on the world. These two signs can form a close and trusting bond: the dog appreciates the rat's intelligence and energy but also understands the rat's watchfulness, and, in return, the rat appreciates the dog's sincerity, honesty and fidelity. In times of trouble, the supportive and trustworthy dog will be at the rat's side, fearlessly offering support.

Rat & Pig

You are both capable of a loving, deep relationship, although the rat's passion may be a bit startling for the pig. The rat can be joyful and intense, meaningful and moody, and the peaceful pig can usually handle the whole range. The pig may be upset if the rat is too aggressive or demanding but usually finds a cheerful way to resolve the tension. The pig shares the rat's sense of fun, and together you both like to indulge in life's luxuries. You are likely to spend many happy and exciting days in each other's company, and although the rat may become frustrated by the pig's innocence, the affection and the care that the pig offers more than compensate for this.

Ox & Ox

You are both good organizers and efficient workers, and it is rare for you to make a hasty judgement. You are not afraid of challenges or variety but you choose security over risk and resent being forced to make rash decisions. Neither of you thrives on turbulent emotional scenes, preferring instead to conduct your relationship at a steady and reliable pace. You know how to find a balance between professional and personal commitments, but, if anything, the pattern of your life may be a little too predictable, and from time to time one of you will be tempted to throw caution to the wind and experiment with the unusual.

Ox & Tiger

The ox has to keep a close eye on the tiger in order for this relationship to flourish. The tiger is able to provide a certain security, which the ox likes, and at the same time adds an air of excitement, which is appreciated as long as it is not pushed too far. In return, the ox is reliable and loving, but should not become too dependent since the tiger also needs freedom. The tiger may get itchy feet and feel the need to flirt and have some fun, and to some extent the ox will try to ignore what is happening. However, the ox does not have limitless amounts of patience; the tiger has to know when to hold back and behave so that the ox can be reassured that all is well.

Ox & Rabbit

You both appreciate the comforts of home and the stability of familiar environments. Neither of you wants to take unnecessary risks or be involved in emotional confrontations; what you need is security, tenderness and dependability. The rabbit is the more hesitant and nervous of the two signs, and if one of you has to defend your relationship then it is the ox who will rise to the challenge. The rabbit is more apprehensive of the unknown or unpredictable, but the ox is well-grounded and solid, armed with common sense and determination when faced by a crisis. And if the ox stubbornly refuses to move from a standpoint, the intelligent rabbit will put the ox at ease and persuade the other to compromise.

Ox & Snake

The ox is attracted by the snake's charm and attentiveness, and will happily care and cater for the beguiling snake. The ox is likely to take care of the domestic organization and finances while the snake ventures forth to pursue new ideas and astutely handle negotiations or deals, returning to the ox now and again for sound advice. When the situation demands, the wise snake rises to a challenge with energy and intelligence; and, when work is over, the ox is welcoming and peaceful company. The ox is trustworthy and patient, and the snake should be careful not to betray this trust, since the foundations are here for a strong partnership.

Ox & Dragon

The ox's patience and orderly life will definitely be challenged by the vivacious dragon. The ox likes to tread cautiously, weighing advantages against disadvantages before making a commitment. The dragon takes more risks, excited by the possibilities ahead but usually intelligent enough to identify the pitfalls. The ox admires the dragon's energy and charisma, while the dragon appreciates the ox's dependability. The ox can provide a stable backdrop to the dragon's adventures, but the dragon must be careful not to take advantage of the ox's support. If the dragon becomes too elusive, the strong-willed ox will be quick to object, so the dragon needs to be open to the concerns of the more conservative ox.

Ox & Horse

It is not always easy for the ox to adapt to the horse's energy and flights of fancy; the horse may head off in direct pursuit of an interesting idea while the ox is still considering the best course of action. The horse's restless nature will eventually irritate the ox, who needs time to sit, reflect and plan. But if the ox is willing to compromise and accept the horse's unusual ideas, the ox may be introduced to some exciting and daring adventures. The ox offers patient and loving support, but the horse cannot expect the ox to make exuberant romantic declarations, and should not be too disappointed when told to act sensibly.

Ox & Ram

In this partnership, the sensible and reliable ox offers the ram stability, and in return the ram is often full of ideas and imaginings that charm the ox. It is likely that the ox will take the responsibility for the day-to-day practicalities and decision-making, which certainly takes a weight off the ram's shoulders. If anything, the ox might be just a little too set in their ways, and this could somewhat dampen the ram's fanciful ideas. However, the ram usually has good intentions and certainly does not want to cause any trouble or harm, and this is appreciated by the ox.

Ox & Rooster

There is plenty of potential here for a happy and long-lasting relationship. Privacy and freedom are important to you both and you also respect each other's talents. The rooster brings fun into the ox's life, introducing new ideas and encouraging the ox to experiment with new colors and designs. The cautious ox enjoys this new dimension, and in return offers reliability and security. The ox may quash some of the rooster's wilder ideas, considering them too frivolous, but will offer support and guidance for the more realistic ones. The ox is steady and dependable, and it is this emotional support that appeals to the vulnerable and sensitive streak that the rooster keeps hidden.

Ox & Monkey

The vivacity of the monkey contrasts to the constancy of the ox. The monkey may be out and about, charming others and colluding in a variety of schemes and projects, while the ox watches with interest but will not try to match the monkey. At the end of the day, the ox provides a stable and firm home base. There is something in the ox's thoroughness that appeals to the monkey, and the ox, who does not play the monkey's games, is not viewed as competition. A level of trust can develop between you both, and as long as the ox is not hurt or deceived, a trusting and balanced relationship can be formed.

Ox & Dog

The ox and the dog share a bond of loyalty, reassured by the fact that they are there for each other at the end of a long day. When troubles appear on the horizon the dog soon becomes anxious, worrying over possible dangers and repercussions, but the ox steadily confronts the problem. Instead of fretting about what is yet to happen, the ox deals sensibly with immediate issues while keeping a watchful eye on the future. When the dog panics, the ox is a calming influence but also appreciates the dog's faithfulness, thoughtfulness and depth of character.

Ox & Pig

The pig likes – and needs – a good social life but is equally content sharing cosy evenings with the ox. The pig appreciates the home-based and stable ox, although will undoubtedly feel restless and convince the ox that a party or a weekend away is just what you both need. Meanwhile, the ox is charmed by the pig's honesty and playful company, and will probably acquiesce to the pig's wishes. From time to time, the ox will be cross when the pig behaves recklessly, perhaps keeping both of you out too late or spending lavish amounts on a luxury item. But, in the end, neither of you wants to upset the other, and it is unlikely that any long-term resentment will be harbored.

Tiger & Rabbit

The tiger is more adventurous than the rabbit, although both share an independent spirit. The tiger's wanderings are likely to be far more lively than those of the rabbit, who prefers time alone to think or to be creative, but ultimately you both want a secure home base. As long as there is versatility and freedom in the relationship you appreciate the times you are together, but neither of you likes to feel trapped. Of the two, it is the tiger who may become restless and wander off in search of new excitement, while the rabbit remains attached to familiar surroundings, so it is important for the tiger to find time at home to share quieter and more intimate moments with the rabbit.

Tiger & Tiger

When two tigers are paired together there will be no shortage of adventure or excitement – if anything, it may work against them. Both have independent and determined natures, both are motivated and active, and it is unlikely that one will want to follow in the other's footsteps. If you are both prepared to allow each other the freedom to pursue personal interests without reporting back to one another, this relationship could work well. You would also have to allow for the fact that domestic life might be rather disorganized, although you might be too busy with other interests to notice!

Tiger & Dragon

This is a combination full of enthusiasm and possibilities. Both characters are spirited and adventurous, although the dragon may give more forethought to a new proposal than the tiger. Both are sociable and open to suggestions and ideas, although if pushed too far it will be hard for the partnership to regain a sense of balance. Routine and predictability are not your strong points – you are more likely to be found in lively argument over some new project or scheme. You are both passionate in your outlook and approach, and your shared enjoyment of life is likely to overcome the disagreements that will inevitably occur.

Tiger & Snake

The tiger who believes something is right or worth fighting for will immediately spring into action. This level of energy and enthusiasm seems unnecessary and often irritating to the snake, who likes to develop a strategy beforehand. While the tiger will try to urge the snake into action, the snake usually prefers to stick to a familiar routine and pace. And although the snake's interest can be aroused by new schemes, it is the way in which the two animal signs operate that may cause antagonism. Like the tiger, the snake is interested in ideas and is capable of identifying social or financial possibilities, but there needs to be compromise and negotiation over the approach.

Tiger & Ram

While the tiger needs independence to pursue new interests, the ram needs independence to contemplate or to dream, with the added requirement for security and reassurance. The ram does not want to be left to fend off strangers, cope with confrontations or be asked to fight for a new cause, and the tiger can provide the security and the care that the ram needs, without making unnecessary demands. The tiger usually knows how far to intercede on the ram's behalf without appearing overprotective. These two signs combine well as they have a mutual respect, but it is important that neither feels trapped in the relationship.

Tiger & Horse

When there is a new place to discover or a party to attend, the tiger and the horse will be there. It takes little persuasion from either side to explore a new avenue or take a risk if there is something interesting to experience. This passion for life is one of the strengths in this relationship, and, even though it can make life chaotic, it does not deter you. While the tiger enjoys adventure for its own sake, the horse is more egotistical and will act because there is something to be gained personally, perhaps without realizing that this is the case. This should not have any kind of detrimental effect on the relationship, however, since the horse believes that the action is done with the best of intentions.

Tiger & Monkey

The adventurous and the astute are combined in this match. You are happy to explore together and experience new situations, but the monkey usually has the upper hand. The tiger may be excitable but is more straightforward than the monkey, so while the monkey is devising schemes and looking at new angles the tiger may be happily traveling along without examining the undercurrents. And while the tiger may be stalled by an unexpected obstacle, the monkey will most likely have already anticipated a way round it. These two animal signs can work well together, but the monkey needs to be more open and less critical, while the tiger needs to be more patient and tolerant.

Tiger & Rooster

The tiger's attention will be caught by the rooster's extrovert character, and for a while this is very appealing, but before long the tiger is likely to criticize rather than flatter. The rooster likes to take an active role in events and is not afraid to comment or to censure, whereas the tiger will begin to question the rooster's judgement. In return, the rooster feels unfairly treated and misrepresented, but beneath the rooster's frank exterior is a responsible and courageous character; it just takes time and understanding for the tiger to appreciate this. In order to put the relationship on a firm footing, both of you must be more patient and truthful about your needs and feelings.

Tiger & Pig

These two signs share many of life's interests and will encourage and defend one another. The bonds of friendship and attraction are likely to be strong; you both recognize the time for companionship and the time for freedom and independence, and will not make unreasonable demands on each other. Sometimes the pig can be naive in their enthusiasms, and the tiger will arrive with a word of warning, which the pig usually accepts. When the tiger heads off in search of adventure the pig will tolerantly watch the tiger from a distance, but when complications arise the pig knows how to rein the tiger back in.

Tiger & Dog

The dog has a more cautious nature than the tiger and will fire a warning shot if they think the tiger is going too far or taking unnecessary risks. In return, the tiger appreciates the dog's watchfulness and loyalty. Sometimes the dog will remain in the background, admiring the tiger's enthusiasm. But if a worthwhile cause presents itself the dog will not hesitate to leap into action. These two animal signs combined create a formidable team when they are fighting on behalf of others. However, while you are both pursuing your individual interests, the tiger should not forget that the dog needs tenderness and reassurance if the relationship is to flourish.

Rabbit & Rabbit

You can find peace, contentment and, above all, harmony in this relationship. While others may enjoy quarrels or unpredictable romantic scenarios, you prefer comfort and reliability, secure in the fact that you have each other. The rabbit needs a familiar environment and likes to be surrounded by beautiful objects and colors to create a world that is welcoming and reassuring. You both enjoy areas of natural beauty, and you also like to explore shops or galleries, buy unusual goods or entertain at home. But the safe world that you create is not prepared for turmoil, and if you are confronted by a crisis it might take all your resources of energy to deal with it and re-establish order once again, so try to keep a sensible eye on the world around you to prepare yourselves for unforeseen events.

Rabbit & Dragon

The rabbit needs security and affection and will withdraw when this balance is threatened. On the other hand, the dragon is an adventurer, driven by challenge and excitement. The rabbit may feel a loss of control, since it is hard to keep track of the dragon and even harder to elicit the regular reassurances that the rabbit needs. However, the rabbit does admire the dragon's confidence, and is happy to retreat into the background when the dragon takes the limelight. The dragon can also be an attentive and charming partner, although this is not consistent enough for the cautious rabbit, who may eventually be forced to confront the dragon; when this happens, the dragon should try to respond gently to the rabbit's emotional needs.

Rabbit & Horse

The horse and the rabbit are capable of great love and tenderness. The horse is passionate and excitable, often carried away by the joy of romance, and the quieter rabbit welcomes these displays of affection and devotion. The rabbit needs to be reassured that they are safe and loved, and the horse is happy to offer this support. The rabbit admires the horse's energy and confidence, although the horse's exuberant nature can make the rabbit withdraw until things have calmed down. But there are also days when the horse feels depressed or isolated, weighed down by the troubles of the world, and the rabbit will be there to offer comfort and sensible advice in this mutually supportive relationship.

Rabbit & Snake

You both relish the opportunity of escaping from the world to find a peaceful corner where you can relax and feel secure in each other's company. You share a love of nature, design and beautiful objects, and days often fly by when you are simply walking or exploring together. The rabbit and the snake need a comfortable base to return to after a day's work, but while you both appreciate privacy it is the rabbit who is most hurt if the home is invaded by strangers or boisterous company. The snake takes more risks and needs challenges, and, unlike the rabbit, is not frightened by sudden change. The rabbit should encourage the snake to be more tolerant, and in return the snake will open the rabbit's eyes to a more exciting world.

Rabbit & Ram

There are times when it seems you have both found a soulmate – and this could be one of them. Together you can go off on flights of fancy, traveling and sharing ideas and experiences. Once the rabbit starts worrying, the ram will calm the other down, while the rabbit demonstrates their appreciation by showing affection and tenderness. In turn, when the ram becomes nervous or hesitant the rabbit will try to offer security. When you both become anxious or unsure at the same time, however, there could be a problem, and this is the weakness in the partnership; you may both be unprepared for unexpected problems and do not have the resources to deal with them. When this happens, you need to stay calm, assess the situation and then work out an effective strategy together.

Rabbit & Monkey

The rabbit is the quieter and more reserved of the two, and although the rabbit can be a dreamer, that does not mean a lack of awareness of the monkey's schemes. The rabbit observes the monkey's comings and goings and usually knows what the monkey has in mind, which – in a subtle way – pleases the monkey. Occasionally, the rabbit needs to curtail the monkey's behavior in case one of them, or even someone else, gets emotionally hurt. The monkey trusts the rabbit's observations and, with a little persuasion, will bow to the rabbit's concerns. But essentially these two signs can grow together to develop an open, intimate and caring partnership.

Rabbit & Dog

The rabbit and the dog are both honorable, honest and reliable. They will not promise more than they can realistically deliver, and are unlikely to put their financial or emotional security at risk. They need reassurance and tenderness, and together they can defend themselves against any intrusions and upheavals. When the dog is anxious, the sensible rabbit will offer comfort, and when the rabbit is frightened, the dog will rise to defend the rabbit. The dog is fiercely protective and can display great courage in the face of a challenge, and when the dog is too outspoken or enraged, the rabbit will find subtle ways to restore the peace.

Rabbit & Rooster

It is going to be hard to find an equilibrium in this match; at times the rooster's energy and drive are too much for the placid rabbit to handle. The rooster's exuberance is in sharp contrast to the normally retiring rabbit, and it will take some careful negotiation to prevent any resentment and recrimination creeping into the relationship. The rabbit needs harmony and is thrown off balance in boisterous company or when confronted by unpredictable behavior. Sometimes the rooster cannot help performing in front of others, although this masks a more thoughtful and reflective nature. The rooster needs to quieten down and trust the rabbit, and in return the rabbit will be able to reach the more sensitive side of the rooster's character.

Rabbit & Pig

There is a peaceful quality to your relationship; it is unlikely that your neighbors would ever hear you arguing, and even more unlikely for you to have a row in public. You have a natural harmony, despite the fact that the pig may play a few pranks or behave outrageously to tease the rabbit. You share a love of the arts and nature, and are happy to spend hours in conversation or wandering around your home, giving each other the space you both appreciate. You can pursue your hopes together, feeling secure in your partnership, and when the pig innocently heads into dangerous waters, the watchful rabbit will usually come to the rescue with a sensible plan.

Dragon & Dragon

When two people of this sign meet, everyone else may be put in the shade by their vitality and charm. You both like to attract attention and be complimented, and it is not unusual for you to have a trail of admirers. Amid your busy schedules you find time to flatter each other before heading off to travel to new places or meet new people. You are rarely overcome by jealousy or a need to be reassured because you are confident of your attraction for one another. You are both full of enthusiasm and like to draw others into your world; if anything, you may miss the fact that you do not have someone to push or give advice to. However, this will not preoccupy you for long since there are so many possibilities for you to explore and share.

Dragon & Horse

You both have an enthusiasm for life and revel in the many opportunities that come your way. You like to travel and explore, perform and be admired, and as long as you have shared interests your energy and excitement will carry you along. Your relationship may hit more turbulent waters when it comes to practicalities, since neither of you wants to deal with the more mundane aspects of life; cracks may also appear in your attitude towards each other, particularly if you begin to make emotional demands. The dragon needs attention and a certain level of devotion, which can make the horse feel trapped. The horse also needs recognition and independence, so you have to be truthful with each other and learn to offer mutual support and admiration.

Dragon & Snake

You both have charm, energy and wisdom and are unlikely to feel intimidated or trapped by one another. The dragon is innately confident and charismatic and enjoys being center stage, and the snake is happy to let the dragon have this moment of glory. The astute and beguiling snake understands the dragon's hopes and fears, judging the appropriate time to congratulate or console. However, there is a possibility that the snake may be too possessive, although both signs have an admiration and respect for each other, recognizing their shared courage and determination. This should ensure that the snake's possessiveness is not a threat to the relationship.

Dragon & Ram

The dragon is able to draw the ram into an exciting and adventurous romance, but while the ram is stimulated by new possibilities it may all happen rather too fast. The ram is more dreamy and whimsical than the dragon, taking time to make a decision and then wandering off to examine something else. The ram does not work at the same pace as the dragon or need the same level of excitement, and while the ram admires the dragon's vivacity and skills they may forget to compliment or congratulate the dragon. In this romance, however, the dragon may find a partner to encourage and cajole, someone who will listen to their dreams and schemes, although there is no guarantee that the ram will actually be paying attention!

Dragon & Monkey

These two are capable of great things and could leave other romances far behind. The dragon is bright, powerful and attractive, but the monkey, knowing how to charm and entice, is not daunted by this. They usually spark off ideas and plans in one another, which makes for a rather imaginative and creative combination. The dragon needs to be admired more than the monkey, and likes to be recognized and praised, and the wily monkey knows just how to do this. The monkey may be charmed but is not blinded by passion or easily fooled. These two signs know exactly how to captivate each other, and together they can make a winning pair.

Dragon & Rooster

The dragon is attracted by the rooster's vivacity and you both share a love of life; together you can inject fun into the most dull situations. The dragon's natural flair and charm attract the rooster, just as the dragon is drawn by the rooster's flamboyance. But you both have a more serious side and are ready to react when your help or advice is needed. You are also responsible in times of trouble. While the dragon has innate confidence and charm, and rarely needs guidance or protection, the rooster needs to share worries and insecurities with a close partner. The weakness of the partnership lies in the fact that the dragon may not always be able to appreciate the rooster's more vulnerable side. But, if you are honest with one another, the dragon will understand and offer support in troubled times.

Dragon & Dog

The dragon's presence could be overwhelming for the watchful dog, who will not be easily convinced by the dragon's plans or won over by the dragon's charms. The dragon is full of energy and ideas, and is not fazed by loud company or unpredictable events. All of this may well make the dog anxious, but it will also annoy the dog and could be a source of argument. The dog wants to know where they stand, but the dragon does not tend to focus on such details. The dog is a faithful, trustworthy partner who enjoys romance but needs security, and the adventurous dragon finds it hard to channel this kind of attention to one person. For this relationship to work, the dog needs to be more adaptable to the dragon's lifestyle, and in return the dragon should offer the dog gentle reassurance.

Dragon & Pig

The bright and gregarious dragon is likely to sweep the pig away in a flurry of romance. The pig loves a social outing and can be entertaining company, but the dragon is usually the center of attention. If a crowd has gathered at a party, it is often the dragon to whom they are drawn, but the pig will not feel abandoned. On the contrary, the pig admires the dragon's flair and they will happily share adventures and exploits together. The pig knows how to congratulate the dragon, to make them feel wanted, and the dragon responds charmingly to the pig's attentions. In return, the dragon does not object to the pig's wanderings or imaginings and is happy to support and encourage the affectionate pig.

Snake & Snake

You admire each other's talents, charm and intelligence, and are happy devising schemes, planning manoeuvres or just relaxing in one another's company. You love discussion and debate, but can also recognize the absurd and share a subtle sense of humor. You can deal with challenges astutely and with determination and will not abandon your goals; but you also sense when the time is right to withdraw. All in all, this relationship has many strong points, although there is also one drawback – you understand each other too well and the thrill of romance might fade. You both have beguiling and determined natures so be careful you do not stifle or oppress one another.

Snake & Ram

Both of you enjoy life's pleasures and do not like being tied to routine. The ram is more dreamy than the snake, although the snake is more likely to join in the ram's wanderings than complain. If circumstances do not suit, the snake will find a subtle way of escaping, and the ram may not even realize it. Having to work together to a strict timetable would put a strain on your relationship; the snake can deal with responsibility and work to deadlines but does not relish it, while the ram feels under pressure to perform. When you are exhausted, neither of you has the energy to provide the comforts you both need, so gauge carefully the level of commitment involved before you accept demanding tasks that may have an effect on your relationship.

Snake & Horse

The horse can easily fall for the snake's charisma and intelligence, and will be excited by the snake's intuitive ideas. The horse needs freedom to roam and explore, and the snake will not object as long as there is no regular request to accompany the horse on these exploits. The snake is a shrewd judge of situations and can subtly control the horse, while the horse is still under the impression of being in charge of the relationship. At times the snake may begin to tire of the horse's boundless enthusiasm and naivety, but when the horse lands in trouble the snake will always be there to offer wise advice. The horse needs admiration and reassurance, which the snake will provide, but both of these signs need the space to pursue their varied interests.

Snake & Monkey

These two have the energy and imagination to deal with several things at once, as long as they are of interest. You both enjoy a challenge and can trigger off ideas in each other, and if needs be you can work well together. The monkey is good at spotting opportunities and figuring a way through difficult situations. But the snake will not be left behind and will adapt to the situation, well aware of what is happening. The snake is more profound than the monkey, prone to examining feelings and actions in depth, and the monkey may lack the patience for these serious discussions. The monkey can be hard to pin down, which can annoy the snake, so at times the monkey may need to be more straightforward to win the snake's confidence.

Snake & Rooster

You share a love of color and design, and are happy shopping with each other or deciding on the right clothes for every occasion. Together you make a very elegant, interesting and lively couple, but your attraction for each other runs deeper than appearances – there is a natural empathy. The rooster may appear superficial but there is a depth of feeling and an intelligence that the wise snake recognizes. The snake is more subtle in thought and action, and the rooster usually has the good sense to accept the snake's wise advice. This relationship has the potential to be open and trusting, since neither of you is afraid to discuss feelings privately, or reveal emotions.

Snake & Pig

The snake likes attention and can impress the pig with amusing stories and displays of skill. Before long, the attentive pig may be revelling in the snake's exploits, and will offer the snake affection and lively company. The snake may be tempted to take advantage of the pig's trust and commitment and wander off, thinking the pig will wait patiently. Indeed, the pig may well be there when the snake returns, but only because the pig has been busy pursuing their own interests. The pig may be fooled once or twice but will soon realize what is happening, and if they should show interest in someone else the snake will be deeply jealous and hurt. These two signs can build a happy relationship, but each needs a little freedom now and again.

Snake & Dog

The affectionate dog trusts and admires the snake's judgement and intuition, and is happy to accept the snake's perceptive advice. When the dog is consumed by anxiety and insecurity, the snake offers the tenderness and reassurance that the dog needs to regain confidence. The dog is rarely jealous of the snake's drive or determination – in fact, the snake will take risks or rise to challenges that would normally make the dog wary or nervous. The dog respects the snake's intelligence and depth, and is a protective, faithful and loving partner in return. The dog rarely curtails the snake's independence but usually remains in the background, offering loyalty and support.

Horse & Horse

Your shared energy and enthusiasm keeps this relationship moving at a fast and sometimes uncontrollable pace. You are both passionate in romance and in life, and when your attention is caught by a new interest you pursue it with vigor. The horse needs freedom to move and explore, and loves discovering new pleasures. You are open and warm-hearted but don't want to face the reality of failure or disappointment, so when your interest wanes you head off in search of new pastures. You need to be liked and reassured, particularly when troubled by inner doubts, but when you are both feeling low you become anxious and withdrawn; use your resources of energy to work through it, or try something new to restore your confidence.

Horse & Ram

The horse is energetic and excitable, always eager to know what is happening somewhere else – and with the energy to join in, too. The ram will go along with the horse, since these new places and faces can add an extra dimension to the ram's imagination. If anything, the horse may be too lively and self-centered, and although rams do not demand continual attention they do need encouragement. If the horse is constantly out and about, when will there be time to notice the ram's hesitancy? More often than not, however, the lack of routine and the unpredictability of this romance serve both partners well.

Horse & Rooster

There could be too many superficial similarities here. You are both aware of your appearance and the impression you create, and need to be recognized and reassured, but in the process you might lose the opportunity to unravel deeper feelings; the competition between you could distract from your underlying needs. The horse is passionate and enthusiastic, often carried along by emotion, but the rooster is more critical, despite sharing some of the horse's impulsive nature. The rooster also has a more practical outlook, and is usually prepared for an emergency. To build this relationship, give each other space to express yourselves, but also make time for quieter moments so you can develop mutual understanding and patience.

Horse & Monkey

The horse is gregarious and open, revealing passions when others are more reticent. At one level, the monkey enjoys the horse's energy and commitment, but this could become too much for the careful monkey. Whereas the monkey plans and calculates, the horse lets emotions flow – the happiness or sadness that they feel is not hidden away. And while the monkey loves romance but is always aware of the pitfalls and possibilities, the horse is more likely to be swept along by the joy of it all. Unless really committed to the relationship, the monkey tends to view this high-powered emotion as unnecessary or inappropriate. But once the monkey understands and appreciates the horse's deeper emotional needs, and the horse, in return, begins to settle down a little, the two signs can build a steadier relationship.

Horse & Dog

The excitable and sociable horse might well find a protective partner in the gentle dog. The horse needs more freedom and excitement than the dog, and while the dog keeps to familiar ground the horse pursues new ideas and discoveries. Sometimes the dog will take a risk and accompany the horse on adventures, but more often than not the generous dog is happy to let the horse take the limelight and be left in peace. Although the horse is prone to sudden anxieties, the dog is the more pessimistic of the two – but often the most practical as well. The dog is a trustworthy and faithful partner to whom the horse can turn for support and reassurance, but the horse should not take advantage of the dog's trust.

Horse & Pig

The horse loves the thrill of romance and delights in displays of emotion, and will express their feelings quite honestly. The pig is happy to reciprocate, and both of you know how to celebrate your good fortune. You both like to explore, travel and make new discoveries, but the pig is willing to let the horse charge ahead and be the focus of attention. The horse can be selfish and forget the pig waiting patiently in the background; sometimes the pig does not mind being overshadowed – welcoming, in fact, the breathing space. The pig needs independence, and the horse has to learn not to demand the kind of continual attention that will limit the pig's freedom and ultimately create resentment.

Ram & Monkey

The astute monkey knows how to enjoy life just as much as the ram, and the two travel well together. If one wants to indulge in a little luxury, then the other is unlikely to refuse, and if a new scheme appears, then both may follow it with enthusiasm. The monkey is clever enough to see what the ram likes and to notice the other's weaknesses or insecurities, and can be a supportive and constructive partner. But the monkey also has an independent and determined streak, and, despite an easygoing front, keeps a close eye on organization and career. The monkey can be diplomatic or political as needed, while the ram may feel adrift in these situations. If the two signs are good friends, however, the monkey will come to the ram's rescue.

Ram & Ram

You have a natural empathy for one another and understand that you need a spiritual dimension to your lives. Many happy days will be spent planning, shopping or traveling, but you do not necessarily demand each other's company. Also, you do not make each other feel hindered because you know that you are both dreamers and need space to pursue your thoughts. The pitfalls in this combination lie in life's practicalities, such as who organizes the house, pays the bills and fulfills family responsibilities. While those around you become increasingly impatient, you wait, hoping that the other partner will act; neither of you wants to be tied to mundane matters, but you will have to reach an agreement whereby you accept certain responsibilities and keep a watchful eye out for possible pitfalls.

Ram & Rooster

From time to time the ram is happy to be in the rooster's limelight, but at heart the ram is much more of a dreamer and idealist. You both enjoy lively company and investigating new interests, but the rooster needs action, is critical of appearances and not afraid to state their thoughts. The ram is less forceful and opinionated, and while the rooster is busy the ram may wander off in pursuit of a new idea. While you share a need for independence, the rooster needs reassurance, whereas the ram is more of a free spirit and may not be able to offer the reliability or security the rooster ultimately needs. The ram will have to focus on supporting the rooster, while the rooster will have to make some allowances for the ram's dreams and ideas.

Ram & Dog

You both have the potential to be interested in the unusual. But the dog will only go so far before worry sets in, while the ram will continue regardless as long as fascination persists. Here lies the difference between you: the dog tends to keep more of a hold on life to avoid becoming anxious and stressed, whereas the ram is sometimes carried away by dreams. However, the ram also has their own fears and insecurities, and if both of you are depressed at the same time you could find yourselves sinking lower and lower if you are not careful. Essentially, you can both be affectionate and caring, and if you add a touch of optimism this should help to carry you through any difficulties.

Monkey & Monkey

There is a meeting of clever minds here; both of you usually know what you want – and how to get it. Monkeys are astute and charming and know how to win others over; and when two monkeys come together they happily captivate each other, fully aware of what they are doing. They play games and they plan, but they do not fool one another. They may tire of each other in favor of someone who is more pliable, but more often than not they thrive in a relationship. They are not prone to great public displays of emotion but they are strong partners who work well together, particularly when they focus on a shared project.

Ram & Pig

The ram and the pig give each other the space to explore their individual interests, and it is unlikely that one will feel trapped by the other. You both appreciate the arts, theatre, film and the finer things in life. If necessary, the pig can offer sensible advice or check that events are not getting out of control, without spoiling the fun in the process. Usually the pig is more in touch with the practicalities of life but will avoid unnecessarily limiting the ram's creative ideas. Both these animal signs share a sensitive nature and find it easy to relate to one another. Also, the pig can usually sense when the ram is either justly upset or being unrealistic, and will find a way to calm these unsettled periods.

Monkey & Rooster

You share a love of the good life and can both be entertaining company, but the rooster is straightforward whereas the monkey is wily. The monkey often has a hidden agenda, which confuses the rooster, who likes to know exactly what is going on and has very direct opinions. The rooster believes in immediate action and is not afraid to speak honestly, but the discerning monkey likes to assess and analyze so that difficulties can be overcome in a more subtle manner. You both need independence, so the best solution is to allow a certain freedom in the relationship and be tolerant with each other, since your contrasting characteristics could complement each other well.

Monkey & Dog

There is a chance that the monkey may prove to be too unpredictable for the sensible dog. While the monkey is ducking and diving, having fun and sorting out projects, the dog may feel unfairly left behind. The dog is more conventional and, although often aware of what is going on, may find it hard to catch up. But these two signs do share a realistic vision of what is happening and can be quite practical when it comes to relationships. They are not likely to throw themselves wildly into passion, and even when in love they maintain their critical faculties. However, the dog may resent or disapprove of the monkey's adept way of handling relationships or escaping from delicate situations. The dog will have to make allowances for the monkey's wily nature, while the monkey should be more open about any plans and schemes.

Rooster & Rooster

Since you share so many of the same qualities, you are able to admire and annoy each other at the same time. You enjoy the luxuries of life, take care of your appearance and like to follow your own routine. If you think something should be said, then you will not hesitate to say it, but your criticisms can be unintentionally hurtful. You are a lively match both for each other and in company, although when you feel the need to state your opinion it might be best to hold back until you have calmed down, since you may regret words said in haste. You are courageous and will come to the aid of those who need you, yet underneath this confident exterior you recognize in one another a more vulnerable and insecure nature and realize that you need to be supportive of each other.

Monkey & Pig

The pig is not easily fooled by the monkey's charms, finding them quite amusing without feeling the need to compete. Although possessing a naive streak, the pig often spots the monkey's tactics and will watch from a distance to see what happens. The pig, however, will not be left in the dark and can also be subtly manipulative if called upon. By nature the pig is more honest and down to earth, but also enjoys having fun and sharing the monkey's gregarious lifestyle. The pig will be a loyal partner, allowing the monkey to have the freedom they need yet remaining constant and providing good company and support.

Rooster & Dog

Both have a sensitive and thoughtful side to their nature, although on the surface the rooster appears outspoken, resilient and independent. The rooster is not afraid of direct action and will speak unashamedly when they feel the truth should be told. The dog is more cautious and nervous, but when confronted by a crisis or faced with an injustice shows courage and strength. The rooster likes to perform and be heard, and the dog can be irritated by this unnecessary flamboyance; it is at times such as this, when you are both angered, that it is easy to hurt each other. But when the rooster's sensitive and serious nature is revealed, the dog will be an understanding and protective partner.

Rooster & Pig

 75

The pig admires the rooster's confidence and social skills but is also able to detect the rooster's more vulnerable side. The rooster appears to be supremely confident, charming in company and straightforward in their opinions, and the pig is happy to share in the fun and entertainment that the rooster provides. Yet the rooster has a deeper and more reflective side that the observant pig can detect, and when they are alone the understanding pig is content to listen to the rooster's concerns. Although you both enjoy a certain level of independence, you also need companionship, and together you can enjoy the highs and lows of life, offering each other mutual support and friendship.

Dog & Pig

 77

These two can learn from each other; the pig can inject fun into the relationship, whereas the dog can offer loyalty and trust. The dog can be suspicious and easily angered, but the pig is sensitive to these moods and will offer tender reassurances. On the other hand, if the pig lands in trouble the dog is there to protect the pig and fight off the troublemakers. They have a good understanding of each other, and when the pig feels the dog is becoming too morose they will devise an imaginative scheme to cheer the dog up. The pig knows when someone is trying to take advantage of the dog, and when the dog is needlessly anxious the forthright pig will soon sort out the problem.

Dog & Dog

 76

You recognize that you both need love, tenderness and security, and together you can enclose yourselves in a safe world. Neither of you wants to be faced by romantic turmoil, unpredictable scenes or financial hardship, and you will work with dedication and energy to protect your relationship and your family. You understand that you can both be anxious and nervous over minor matters or about the future, and may spend hours discussing your worries, but at least you respect each other's emotions and opinions. You are able to maintain a strong partnership, and when you are actually faced by a crisis or witness unfair circumstances you have the courage and commitment to rise to the challenge.

Pig & Pig

 78

This relationship will certainly have its tempestuous moments but it also promises great things. You know and understand each other; you both like freedom but not all the time, and you love activity but also need peace. Fortunately, you know one another well enough to gauge these moods, although when you are both in a determined or excited frame of mind it could cause rifts. You are not likely to dwell on arguments for too long because there are so many things to do and to share. Perhaps you know each other too well, and although you are very honest and affectionate you do occasionally need to outwit each other to create a challenge as well as to inject a note of fun into the partnership.

3 The sixty-year CYCLE

Chinese time is traditionally measured in sixty-year cycles formed by the interaction of the ten Heavenly Stems and the twelve Earthly Branches, the ancient astrological systems that were mapped against all cycles of human activity and natural phenomena.

The significant role that the sixty-year cycle commands in Chinese culture is indisputable. For instance, there are sixty gods traditionally associated with the cycle; these are enshrined in Chinese temples, and every year a god takes center stage. People bring offerings such as fruit and flowers and burn incense, and also place money into the lap of their birth god. Amulets of the birth god can be bought for protection and prosperity.

In this chapter, you will discover how your position within the sixty-year cycle has influenced your life, according to the *variation* of animal to which you belong. Each animal appears five times within the cycle in a slightly different form: 1934 was the Year of the Dog on Guard, for example, but 1970 was the Year of the Temple Dog. These readings offer an extra dimension to your overall personality picture, and reveal how it is possible for different fortunes to befall two people of the same animal sign.

HEAVENLY STEMS AND EARTHLY BRANCHES

The ten Heavenly Stems and twelve Earthly Branches are closely linked in Chinese astrology and interact with each other, representing the meeting of heaven and earth.

But they also have a much wider role in Chinese divination, since they have far-reaching associations with other branches of traditional Chinese arts and sciences. These include, among other things, the five elements that make up the universe, the directions of the compass and the seasons, as well as the more specific measures of time such as hours, days, months and years. In addition, the Earthly Branches are linked to the twelve animal signs; the tables shown here demonstrate just some of the universal phenomena with which they are associated.

The Heavenly Stems and the Earthly Branches repeat in sequence in a continuous cycle, pairing up with each other to give sixty different variations in total (see circular chart opposite). The sixty-year cycle always begins with the Heavenly Stem *Chia* and the Earthly Branch *Tzu*, the stems repeating six times and the branches five times before the pairing of *Chia* and *Tzu* comes up once again, marking the new beginning of the sixty-year cycle.

Up until the twentieth century the Chinese calendar was measured according to this cycle of sixty years. For example, 1815 was the year *Yi Hai* in the reign of the Emperor Chia-ch'ing. Although this dating system ceased to be used officially after China was declared a republic in 1912, it is still widely consulted for assessing years in astrological charts.

HEAVENLY STEMS	ASSOCIATIONS INCLUDE		
	Element	Color	Taste
Chia	wood	green	sour
Yi	wood	green	sour
Ping	fire	red	bitter
Ting	fire	red	bitter
Mou	earth	yellow	sweet
Chi	earth	yellow	sweet
Keng	metal	white	acrid
Hsin	metal	white	acrid
Jen	water	black	salt
Kuei	water	black	salt

EARTHLY BRANCHES	ASSOCIATIONS INCLUDE		
	Animal	Season	Direction
Tzu	rat	midwinter	N
Ch'ou	ox	late winter	NNE
Yin	tiger	early spring	ENE
Mao	rabbit	mid-spring	E
Ch'en	dragon	late spring	ESE
Szu	snake	early summer	SSE
Wu	horse	midsummer	S
Wei	ram	late summer	SSW
Shen	monkey	early autumn	WSW
Yu	rooster	mid-autumn	W
Hsu	dog	late autumn	WNW
Hai	pig	early winter	NNW

FINDING YOUR ANIMAL TYPE

Each pairing of Heavenly Stem and Earthly Branch represents a particular variation of one of the twelve animals. For example, if you were born in the Year of the Ox, there are personality traits that belong to your sign regardless of the specific type of ox associated with your year. So the Ox in the Sea may share most of the characteristics of the Ox in the Lake, but there may be certain differences when it comes to forecasting family relationships, future prosperity and job prospects.

In order to find out which animal type applies to you, you need to know your number in the sixty-year cycle. Turn to the lunar chart listed on pages 118–27 to find out the number that applies to the year in which you were born, and then find this number along the outer edge of the circular chart shown below. Next to this number you will find the Heavenly Stem and the Earthly Branch for your year in the cycle; you can then turn to the page with the readings for your animal sign to discover the character attributes and fortune that your type of animal brings to your life.

KEY

FIRST WORD OF PAIR = Heavenly Stem for year
SECOND WORD OF PAIR = Earthly Branch for year

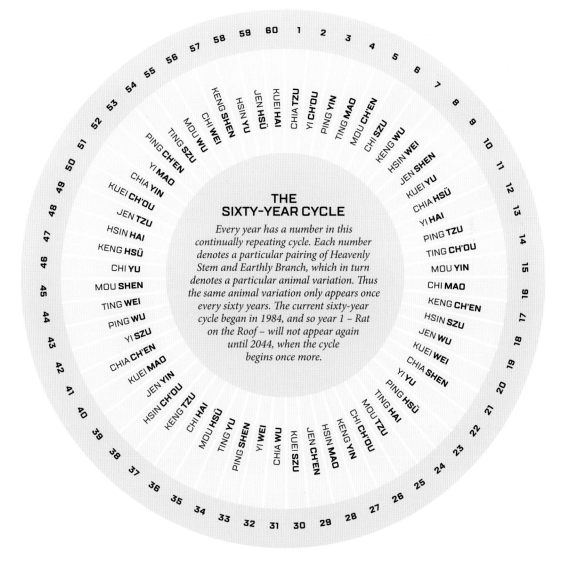

THE SIXTY-YEAR CYCLE

Every year has a number in this continually repeating cycle. Each number denotes a particular pairing of Heavenly Stem and Earthly Branch, which in turn denotes a particular animal variation. Thus the same animal variation only appears once every sixty years. The current sixty-year cycle began in 1984, and so year 1 – Rat on the Roof – will not appear again until 2044, when the cycle begins once more.

Rat

CHIA TZU YEAR
Rat on the Roof
You are intelligent and alert to new opportunities but also easily distracted. Your impatience to explore new avenues may affect your attention to detail; you can leave projects unfinished, hoping others will complete them. In your early career you need to be self-reliant, as others may be unable to offer support.

PING TZU YEAR
Rat in the Field
Your energy and drive can be overwhelming, and while many are impressed others find you hard to handle. You can be too impatient with those less confident than you; try to be more tolerant. You are an intelligent and careful worker, best suited to jobs with an element of competition rather than diplomacy.

MOU TZU YEAR
Rat in the Warehouse
You are pleasant and bright, know how to adapt in unexpected circumstances and are at ease in most social situations. But domestic affairs make you nervous, and your anxious concerns for your family could create tensions, particularly if you have children. You do, however, have a trusting nature, so try to relax and focus on the more positive aspects of family life.

KENG TZU YEAR
Rat on the Beam
You combine sincerity with strong will, and in times of crisis prove to be a supportive and constant friend. You are perceptive and realistic and rarely let inappropriate emotions affect your judgement – and you can easily handle organizational challenges thanks to your excellent management skills.

JEN TZU YEAR
Rat on the Mountain
Although you appear to be cheerful and lively, there is an anxious side to your character that others rarely see. When under pressure you often feel it is inappropriate to discuss your own worries, and problems can weigh you down. Try to share your feelings with others who can offer you the support you need.

YI CH'OU YEAR

Ox in the Sea

You are excited by new discoveries and open to innovative projects. Your steady interest in the world around you and enthusiasm for life makes you a popular companion. You also have an innate charm combined with a dependability that draws a wide circle of friends who will be there in times of trouble.

TING CH'OU YEAR

Ox in the Lake

You are sympathetic to those in need, but in your enthusiasm to support worthy causes or fund interesting projects you may suddenly find that your finances have run dangerously low. However, your generosity is usually returned and you are unlikely to find yourself in desperate financial straits.

CHI CH'OU YEAR

Ox Inside the Gate

You have a candid and open nature but sometimes speak without due thought and, inadvertently, offend others. Although you are a reliable team worker, you are ideally suited to working independently or to running your own business. You are never likely to be short of work, but you may find that you need to seek financial support in order to fulfill your ideas.

HSIN CH'OU YEAR

Ox on the Way

You have a flexible and warm manner, which puts people at ease, and when you find yourself in uncomfortable situations you assess what is happening to avoid further complications. You approach dilemmas sensibly, aware that problems are more likely to be resolved through negotiation rather than force.

KUEI CH'OU YEAR

Ox Outside the Gate

You are a skilled and dedicated worker but your steady efforts may not be appreciated straight away. However, lack of recognition will not deter you from your aims; you know from experience that it just takes time and patience to achieve your goals. Persevere, and many of your hopes will be realized.

Tiger 虎

PING YIN YEAR
Tiger in the Forest

You are observant, quickly absorbing important facts, and this gives you the confidence to speak out on any issue. But if the conversation turns to subjects you consider irrelevant, it is hard for others to hold your attention. You may be restless but your intentions are sincere, and you are a committed friend.

MOU YIN YEAR
Tiger Crossing the Mountain

You react strongly to situations; when things go according to plan, you are quick to congratulate those concerned, but when problems appear, you panic. You enjoy challenges but become unsettled if trapped in situations beyond your control. Be patient and solutions will soon become apparent.

KENG YIN YEAR
Tiger Descending the Mountain

You are tough, hard-working and generous. Like many tigers, you are prone to mood swings and will complain vigorously if you feel insulted or deceived. But your anger is short-lived and you are naturally forgiving, rarely holding grudges for long. Friends and relations appreciate your energy and care, and you are likely to have a supportive family.

JEN YIN YEAR
Tiger Passing Through the Forest

You are thoughtful and intelligent but speak directly and candidly. While some admire your outspoken approach, others can find it inappropriate or upsetting. Your intentions are genuine, however, and when an important issue is at stake you feel that it is your duty to speak your mind.

CHIA YIN YEAR
Tiger Standing Still

You are a good observer, and before making a commitment you take time to consider the possibilities of success or failure. As long as you are stimulated by your work, you are happy to accept responsibility, and your determination and caution make you an adaptable and intelligent colleague and friend.

Rabbit 兔

TING MAO YEAR
Rabbit Looking at the Moon
You have great endurance, rarely letting anything drag you down. You know that if you allow yourself to mull over setbacks it could have far-reaching effects, so you work enthusiastically to create a good ambience. You apply the same dedication to your work, although at times you can be overexcitable.

CHI MAO YEAR
Rabbit Running out of the Forest
You do not want to stand out from the crowd or face the challenge of large-scale organizing or decision-making. You like to work within hierarchies where you are sure of your role, without the anxiety of being responsible for unexpected problems. Once you feel secure, you should have a fruitful career.

HSIN MAO YEAR
Rabbit in the Burrow
On the surface, you create a carefree and energetic impression, but those close to you know that you find it hard to shrug off your worries. Unfamiliar people and new environments make you nervous, so you speak without forethought. However, you are sincere and have an innate strength, and in safe surroundings you regain your confidence and courage once more.

KUEI MAO YEAR
Rabbit Running in the Forest
You have a happy outlook on life, and luck seems to be on your side. With the help of someone who has the power and authority to be of assistance, misfortunes that befall you are often transformed into opportunities. While this may not bring financial gain, in time you will establish the security you need.

YI MAO YEAR
Buddha Rabbit
You have natural charm and energy, and although you feel it is important to achieve some level of success and wealth, there is also a more caring side to your character. You are organized and quietly determined and like to see justice done – even if it means compromising your career or your income.

Dragon 龙

MOU CH'EN YEAR
Yielding Dragon
You have a distinctive character and notable presence, and although you may appear intimidating you are essentially thoughtful and accommodating. Your willingness to adapt to situations is appreciated by others, but be careful that more forceful colleagues do not take advantage of your amenable nature.

KEN CH'EN YEAR
Angry Dragon
You are confident, able and determined but also aware of your talents, and there may be times when your pride is used against you. You do have natural charisma and presence, but on occasion you need to recognize that others have different strengths and need to be approached with more sensitivity.

JEN CH'EN YEAR
Dragon in the Rain
You are an industrious and intelligent worker, but this may well be put to the test early on in your life. You have the courage to face challenges and are rarely disheartened, but if you find that problems are getting on top of you do not be disillusioned, as you have the necessary resources ultimately to overcome any obstacles in your way.

CHIA CH'EN YEAR
Cheerful Dragon
You are a good judge of situations and feel that justice should be carried out, even if it means putting your reputation on the line. You keep a clear distinction between your professional and personal life and are a dependable and efficient worker, rarely allowing career worries to affect your family life.

PING CH'EN YEAR
Dragon Flying to Heaven
You are intelligent and energetic, and rarely tire of meeting new people or experiencing new places. The thrill of travel spurs you on; you need to have the freedom to sense the color and variety of life, and it may be a long time before you feel you can commit yourself to one person or place.

Snake 蛇

CHI SZU YEAR
Prosperous Snake

You are a diligent and perseverant worker, and most projects flourish under your guidance. You analyze situations carefully and are a sharp judge of character, which serves you well in your career. Outside the workplace, your determined approach mellows, to be replaced by a more gentle, caring disposition.

HSIN SZU YEAR
Snake Sleeping in the Winter

You have an ambitious nature combined with intelligent originality, but it may be hard for you to establish your reputation or commit yourself to one career. Your early working life may be unpredictable, but you handle finances wisely and can look forward to more prosperous years ahead.

KUEI SZU YEAR
Snake in the Grass

You are astute in your observations and deft in your actions. This quick-witted approach will undoubtedly serve you well at work, but do not assume that there will always be a guaranteed income. Keep watch on your financial commitments – your inclination to spend money as quickly as you earn it may create tensions in your personal relationships.

YI SZU YEAR
Snake Coming out of the Hole

You are industrious, honest and popular, though the contributions you make are not always recognized. You sometimes underplay your efforts, but this self-effacing approach means you do not always receive due praise or financial reward; in time, your endeavors will finally be acknowledged.

TING SZU YEA
Snake in the Fish Pond

You are determined to achieve your goals and may use unconventional methods to do so. Your tough, decisive approach rarely allows obstacles to stand in your way, but it may alienate others who do not share your vision. Your dedication, however, is appreciated by those on behalf of whom you are working.

Horse 马

KENG WU YEAR
Horse in the Hall

You are honest and straightforward, but in your eagerness to express opinions you may sometimes appear tactless. You are a loyal and dedicated partner and parent, always ready to help or defend your family. When those close to you have been hurt, you lay your own concerns aside to help them.

JEN WU YEAR
Horse in the Army

Your hard and dedicated approach to work will provide you with financial stability, and though you appreciate life's comforts you rarely waste money on unnecessary items. You are lively, amenable company but you also have an independent streak and expect others not to interfere in your personal matters.

CHIA WU YEAR
Horse in the Clouds

You are thoughtful and quick to react in defence of those who cannot fight for themselves. Your optimistic nature allows you to cope with financial hardships in the belief that good fortune will soon be on the way, while your compassionate nature provides you with supportive friends, ready to help you in difficult times, just as you have helped them.

PING WU YEAR
Horse on the Way

You are not short of dedication or energy, but it may take longer than imagined for your goals to be realized. You are an understated leader who can inspire others with ease, but your personal relationships are often more complex, due to your emotional enthusiasm, though your commitment will be appreciated.

MOU WU YEAR
Horse Within the Gate

You are warm-hearted with a sympathetic and gentle personality that endears you to many. You are stimulated by new opportunities and approach them with enthusiasm and intelligence. It may take time, but through such exploration you will eventually discover the interests that suit your nature.

Ram 羊

HSIN WEI YEAR
Prosperous Ram

You are an idealistic person, ready to trust and forgive those who have hurt you. Although your gentle nature endears you to many, it also makes you vulnerable to manipulation or deceit. However, before you realize what is happening, your friends usually spot potential exploitation and guard you against it.

KUEI WEI YEAR
Ram in a Flock of Sheep

You are generous and open-hearted, ready to give time and money to worthy causes. However, you sometimes express yourself in a tactless or outspoken way, which obscures the efforts you have made. But when you believe in an issue you are not easily deterred, and in time your efforts will be appreciated.

YI WEI YEAR
Ram Respected by Others

You are an industrious and honest worker who inspires respect and trust among colleagues and friends. You appreciate the value of money and would make an efficient manager, as long as you are given a certain amount of freedom to express your opinions and experiment with new ideas. You will find that your hard work is likely to reap financial rewards in due course.

TING WEI YEAR
Lonely Ram

You can be subject to sudden mood swings. Sometimes you are inspired by the possibilities ahead of you and at other times saddened by the events you witness or by news that you hear. You feel it is important to know the truth, and you will steadily seek answers through investigation or debate.

CHI WEI YEAR
Ram Running on the Mountain

You are an excellent debater, skilfully acknowledging the points your opponent makes, while firmly presenting your own. Your character is straightforward, combined with a natural elegance and charm; you are not afraid to pass judgement but usually do so in a way that does not cause unnecessary offence.

Monkey 猴

JEN SHEN YEAR
Elegant Monkey
You are bright and gregarious but prone to unexpected mood swings that can dampen your spirits. You need the assurance of being financially secure, which can at times make you over-thrifty, and though you are generous with friends and family you may skimp on repairs or waste time in search of a bargain.

CHIA SHEN YEAR
Monkey Climbing a Tree
You have a strong and charming presence that attracts friends with ease. Your witty and clever conversation soon draws out the feelings of others, but you reveal little of yourself in the process. You also have a resolute nature and can usually survive complex emotional and political situations.

PING SHEN YEAR
Monkey Climbing the Mountain
Your astute and intelligent mind allows you skilfully and easily to piece together a picture of events from the most minor of clues, and then assess the situation accordingly. You are also a sound judge of character and are rarely deceived by others. With these combined traits you are well suited to a career in business or law.

MOU SHEN YEAR
Lonely Monkey
You are impatient and busily dart from issue to issue exploring what is happening and who is involved. Your emotions change quickly but you rarely let mood swings distract you from your work. You have good insight into the motives that drive those around you and are a thorough and dedicated worker.

KENG SHEN YEAR
Monkey in a Fruit Tree
You are likely to be stylish and fashionable, paying attention to the company you keep and the appearance you create. You are bright and shrewd and have an active nature, but sometimes you should be less forceful; give yourself time to quietly observe what is happening and then react to the situation.

Rooster 鸡

KUEI YU YEAR
Rooster in the Hen Roost

You like to see justice done and are straightforward in your opinions. You approach life enthusiastically, and when you hear a secret your eagerness to share it makes it hard to resist telling others. You can negotiate your way through problems, even though your family may be unable to offer support.

YI YU YEAR
Singing Rooster

You expect the best of people and circumstances, and your optimistic streak makes you believe things will work out well in the end, even if this is unlikely. You like to step in with your thoughts and opinions, but, though well intentioned, it might be better to hold back and wait for events to unravel.

TING YU YEAR
Lonely Rooster

You are sociable and cheerful, usually quick to make friends in the most unexpected places, many of whom may prove to be influential in your life. There is a sentimental side to your character and you are moved by emotional events. You also have a lucky streak, and despite the fact that your youth may have its share of problems your fortune increases as the years pass by.

CHI YU YEAR
Rooster Announcing the Dawn

Luck is on your side, especially in relation to finance, although your family relationships may have unpredictable highs and lows. You have a good understanding of what others are thinking, but despite this your behavior can be erratic and may unintentionally hurt others, so try to be more careful in your actions.

HSIN YU YEAR
Rooster in a Cage

You have the will to succeed, combined with an active and relatively healthy constitution, and you like to be involved in the heart of a project rather than be an onlooker. You are stimulated by new ideas and ready to participate in discussions, where your debating skills are both appreciated and respected.

Dog 狗

CHIA HSÜ YEAR
Dog on Guard

You are a skilled negotiator, rarely backing down or acknowledging defeat, although your stubborn streak can turn personal discussions into arguments. You enjoy the rush of daily life, but you also have a contemplative side to your nature and give more thought to serious matters than others may imagine.

PING HSÜ YEAR
Sleepy Dog

Your relaxed nature will serve you well in your career, since you allow time for other people, helping them to deal with personal or professional dilemmas. You cannot, however, work efficiently when forced to make decisions or asked to meet tight deadlines, so avoid careers in which this is an integral aspect.

MOU HSÜ YEAR
Dog Going Into the Mountain

You have an independent nature and prefer to rely on your own judgement, although this does not make you any less generous or thoughtful when others seek your advice. The intuitive side of your character enables you to spot potential trouble or act on positive opportunities, and it also helps you to understand the motives that drive other people.

KENG HSÜ YEAR
Temple Dog

You are generally content with life and your fortune, and rarely force your opinions or needs onto others. But you also have a strong and determined reserve of character, which emerges when you are confronted by an injustice or witness unfair treatment, and you are swift to rise to the challenge.

JEN HSÜ YEAR
Family Dog

It is hard for you to hold on to money for long, since you either spend it on your family or on worthy causes. Although your financial fortunes may fluctuate, your generosity creates its own momentum among friends and colleagues, and it will not be forgotten when you are in need of help.

Pig

YI HAI YEAR
Pig Passing By

You are honest in your dealings and straightforward in your opinions, but your outspoken approach may create tensions with older members of your family. You may be more comfortable sharing your feelings with those outside your family circle. In time, your problems will ease and you will feel more settled.

TING HAI YEAR
Pig Passing the Mountain

You have an alert and enthusiastic nature, happy to explore new interests and quick to spot the potential in unlikely situations. You are not frightened by challenging projects, but you do take your personal commitments into consideration before accepting work to avoid it interfering with your family life.

CHI HAI YEAR
Monastery Pig

You are optimistic and alert, and have the confidence to carry you through the unexpected; when circumstances change, you try to find a way to adapt your plans accordingly. You seem to have the good fortune of being in the right place at the right time, combined with the intelligence to recognize the opportunities you are given and make the most of them.

HSIN HAI YEAR
Pig in the Garden

You focus on the issues that affect you and those close to you, rarely interfering with anyone else. You recognize that people need privacy, and although you are ready to offer support you usually only do so when invited. You also value your independence and are confident in your decisions and outlook.

KUEI HAI YEAR
Pig in the Forest

You form close friendships and, in times of trouble, can be relied upon to come to the defence of friends or share their sorrows. You have a strong sense of purpose combined with determination bordering on obstinacy, but once you have made a promise you keep your word and work with dedication and skill.

4 Hours, days
AND MONTHS

In Chinese astrology, forecasts can be made on a number of different levels. You have already discovered your fortune according to the animal sign for the year in which you were born, and found out how the sixty-year cycle has influenced your character. But your fortune is also accountable to the hour, day and month of your birth, as you will soon discover in this chapter.

The readings for the hours and the days apply to all the animal signs and provide a general guide to the personality traits with which they are associated. The readings for the months, however, are particular to each of the twelve animal signs and offer additional insight into your character, relating to the lunar month in which you were born. Since the readings for these aspects are based on such precise birth details, this enables you to add a further personal dimension to your overall horoscope picture. Remember that it is up to you to make the most of the advice given; simply being *aware* of any negative traits associated with your forecast will help you to deal with them on a day-to-day basis and thus could change your life for the better.

YOUR CHINESE HOUR OF BIRTH

In Chinese astrology the day is broken down into twelve hours, each one corresponding to two Western hours. The first recorded evidence of the twelve hours appears on a Chinese calendar dating back to the fifth century BCE, although such a division of the day is thought to predate this calendar.

The twelve hours are named after the Earthly Branches, which means that they also correspond to the twelve animal signs (see also page 60). Check the table below to see which two-hour period includes your time of birth (if you were born on the cusp of a Chinese hour, such as 3am, refer to the earlier reading). Traditionally, the reading for your hour of birth is considered to be an "extra" reading that may be given by a fortune-teller to provide additional general information.

Chinese hours	Earthly Branches	Animal
11pm–1am	Tzu	Rat
1am–3am	Ch'ou	Ox
3am–5am	Yin	Tiger
5am–7am	Mao	Rabbit
7am–9am	Ch'en	Dragon
9am–11am	Szu	Snake
11am–1pm	Wu	Horse
1pm–3pm	Wei	Ram
3pm–5pm	Shen	Monkey
5pm–7pm	Yu	Rooster
7pm–9pm	Hsu	Dog
9pm–11pm	Hai	Pig

TZU HOURS 11pm–1am

You are hot-tempered and sometimes dive into a situation without forethought, only to regret it afterwards; your hasty actions can make you a target for gossip. With time and experience, you will find a more level approach to life. Though you are most suited to an independent working life, your family will be there to offer support.

CH'OU HOURS 1am–3am

In your youth it may be hard to achieve the freedom or career you aim for, and you may have to leave familiar surroundings in order to pursue your interests. At times it may seem that circumstances conspire against you, but your fortune will improve as the years pass.

YIN HOURS 3am–5am

Your relationship with your family may be troubled when you are younger, and family disagreements make it difficult for you to pursue your particular interests. As you grow older, these problems are likely to fade into the background, and your fortune will take a strong turn for the better after the age of forty.

MAO HOURS 5am–7am

Good fortune shines on you from an early age, and this is improved further with help from your parents, although you may not always receive the support you need from other members of your family. Your romantic life will be unpredictable in your twenties and early thirties but will settle down in the following years.

CH'EN HOURS 7am–9am

You are clever, quick-witted and good company. Your positive outlook on life enables you to form close friendships, and as a result your life can be as busy and as varied as you choose to make it. You have to take care not to be overconfident, though your optimism and determination will usually see you through.

SZU HOURS 9am–11am

You are organized, thorough and attentive to the tasks you are given, with a good head for running a business, and you are happy to share the fruits of your success with family and friends. Your weaknesses are your extravagance and a tendency to overindulge, but this is compensated by a kind, thoughtful side to your nature.

WU HOURS 11am–1pm

You are intelligent and active but you can also be obstinate and resist change, even though you know others may be right. At times you may have to give in to keep the peace or resolve situations. You need to explore opportunities and prefer the freedom to travel over a regular job in a familiar environment.

WEI HOURS 1pm–3pm

Your youth may be troubled by arguments and disagreements within your family or in your romantic life, but these upsets will gradually be resolved as time passes. You have an active and questioning spirit and find it hard to focus your attentions on one job, but in many ways it is this enquiring approach that will impress others.

SHEN HOURS 3pm–5pm

You have a lucky streak and find it easy to make money, but you are also extravagant and enjoy going on spending sprees – though fortunately you are never likely to find yourself down and out. You need to give time to problems that appear in your romantic life, but do not lose touch with the demands of your career in the process.

YU HOURS 5pm–7pm

You may have to leave familiar surroundings in search of further training or a career, although this does not mean that you will lose contact with your family. Wherever you go you settle well because you are open to new friendships, adaptable to new environments and careful not to betray confidences.

HSU HOURS 7pm–9pm

You are extremely capable and optimistic, and courageously rise to the challenge of running your own business or working alone. Although you appreciate the importance of financial rewards, it is variety and opportunity that give you the will to continue.

HAI HOURS 9pm–11pm

You are manually skilled and are likely to have a natural talent for handicrafts. Once you have an idea, you energetically pursue it until it is realized. It is not your style to abandon something halfway through or hand something over without having done the finishing touches.

YOUR CHINESE DAY OF BIRTH

The readings for the days fall into nine different groups. Each group is made up of three or four days, all of which are nine days apart from one another.

This grouping into numbers of nine holds the same significance as do the Nine Stars in Chapter Five, corresponding to the trigrams that make up every aspect of the universe (see page 110 for further explanation).

To find out the lunar day on which you were born, you will need to turn to the lunar chart at the back of the book (see page 118). Follow the instructions on how to calculate your day of birth, and then return to this section to see what your reading has in store.

1st · 10th · 19th · 28th

You set high standards for yourself and others and you will fight to achieve them. You are an independent and trustworthy person, but your determination does sometimes overrule the concerns of others, and in an effort to complete projects quickly you may create more problems. Try to be more cautious and careful. You are suited to work in public life in the areas of law, management and the planning of social affairs.

3rd · 12th · 21st · 30th

You are sensitive to the world around you and quick to defend a just cause. You have a disciplined approach to work and a good head for business, combined with a strong competitive element. Although people may initially be wary of approaching you, since they wrongly assume that you are stern or difficult, once they come to know you they will realize that you have a natural concern for others.

2nd · 11th · 20th · 29th

You know how to enjoy life, and your open, honest approach makes you popular. But there is also a quieter side to your nature, when you prefer to be left alone to think or read. You know how to make the most of situations but need to learn to control your temper when you are under pressure. You are suited to a career as a designer, literary editor or planner.

4th · 13th · 22nd · 31st

You have a reserved nature and a calm approach to life, although this sometimes works against you as people may mistakenly assume that you are cold or even unapproachable. In fact, you are patient and open, and more than willing to offer support if you are asked. You are suited to research work or an academic career, particularly in theology or philosophy.

7th · 16th · 25th

You enjoy life and are happy to go in search of lively company or exciting opportunities. You are often so busy performing or revelling in the moment that you lose contact with reality, and so it is important that you apply a certain level of discipline in your life. You are suited to a job that gives you the freedom to travel, investigate and explore.

5th · 14th · 23rd

You use your intelligence well but have a fiery nature, which makes it difficult for you to accept advice from others. It takes a great deal of persuasion to make you change your mind, and along the way you could miss out on possible opportunities. You are a good initiator, suited to a career as an administrator, an academic or a designer.

8th · 17th · 26th

You have a calm nature and are a good judge of character and of circumstances, quietly observing what is happening around you. You have a determined and logical approach to life, and when at work you feel more comfortable pursuing projects on your own than as part of a team. Your fortune throughout life will be varied; you tend to go where the spirit takes you, and along the way you will encounter times of hardship but also times of wealth.

6th · 15th · 24th

You have an open and cheerful character, which attracts many friends. Your intentions are good but your willingness to come to the aid of others is often hampered by your indecisiveness: even though your heart is in the right place, your daydreaming sometimes prevents you from fulfilling your promises. You are suited to work in creative fields as an artist or designer or in projects that involve working on behalf of others, as long as you are not put under too much pressure.

9th · 18th · 27th

You have an optimistic and open character, welcoming new opportunities and experiences. You have a happy outlook on life, and it is rare for you to be troubled by minor matters. One of your weaknesses is your unpredictable changes of mood, and, while you are generally good company, you can be quarrelsome over unexpected matters. You are suited to a job which gives you a degree of independence.

YOUR CHINESE MONTH OF BIRTH

As the Chinese months correspond to the lunar cycle, you need to know which lunar month your birth date falls into in order to refer to the relevant reading.

You should have already discovered your lunar month when calculating your lunar day of birth, but if you need to remind yourself simply turn to the lunar chart on pages 118–27 and check which lunar month corresponds to your day of birth. The readings for the lunar months are particular to each animal sign, and can be found on the following pages.

You are straightforward and serious in your approach to life, and friends appreciate your earnest nature. You do not, however, like to feel trapped or make long-term career commitments unless you know there is some means of escape. You keep your cool in a crisis, and it is not unusual for people to turn to you for help. But sometimes your controlled nature may be a hindrance, so you should learn to express your hidden emotions and sense of humor more frequently.

You have good intuition and can put your talents to effective use – at times, everything you touch seems to blossom. But do not overestimate your own abilities or assume things will work out as planned; your complacency may lead you into deeper trouble than you can handle. You are clever but also sensitive, and when you apply these skills they serve you well. You can enchant others with ease but can also upset others without realizing, so try not to act too hastily in delicate situations.

You are accessible and popular but few people realize that you are also shy and emotional. To the outsider you seem to run your life – and particularly your career – with authority and determination, but underneath you worry about the progress and outcome of your efforts. Do not subject yourself to undue pressure; there is no need, since your apparent drive and efficiency will attract attention and subsequent opportunities.

You have a generous and extravagant nature, which makes you a popular host and guest, but you are also a good, careful organizer. Before making a commitment, you thoughtfully assess the situation, because once you have given your word you will not go back on it. You can be relied upon to approach work thoroughly and rarely let any obstacle stand in your way, yet at the same time you are also open to advice from others and will act on it readily.

You are able to deal with life sensibly and positively, but the thrill of romance can distract you from life's practicalities. Friends and romantic partners are drawn by your cheerfulness and charm, but you are also outspoken and your well-intentioned criticisms may sometimes cause offence. You have a buoyant nature, however, and although the end of a friendship or relationship may leave you feeling depressed it will not be long before you find a new partner.

You are optimistic and full of original ideas, and can usually spot a good opportunity in unfavorable circumstances. Although you are extravagant, spending freely on yourself and others, your ability to recognize the potential in unlikely situations will ultimately prove to be profitable. While good luck generally seems to be on your side, you must try not to be overconfident as there is a chance that your intuition may fail you at a crucial moment.

You approach life carefully, aware of what other people think or want, and adapt your behavior accordingly. You may even be too attentive to detail and could find it hard to form close friendships as a result. You are watchful in your dealings: you do not take advantage of others, or let them take advantage of you. Despite your normal discretion, a gregarious side of your nature emerges in your personal relationships, when you find it easier to relax and develop a sense of trust.

You are attentive and intuitive and can quickly assess – and react to – situations. Your ability to perceive the motives that drive others not only enables you to cultivate strong friendships but can also prove profitable in financial negotiations. You are understanding of other people's problems and do everything you can to help your friends through difficult periods. You also thrive in situations that involve an element of risk and enjoy the excitement of a new challenge.

You are sensitive to the world around you and ready to forgive others or lend an understanding ear to those who need you. This can be interpreted as a clever move on your part, but you do have a genuine concern for others. There is also a disciplined, alert side to your character, and once you are in a stable working environment you apply your skills with determination and energy. Although you are likely to have many friends, there are few with whom you share your innermost thoughts.

It may take many years of dedicated work before your skills are finally recognized, but you are an efficient planner and determined worker. You are perceptive and rarely disturbed by unforeseen obstacles, although at first others may not appreciate these attributes, since they assume you are too emotional. You can easily access complex situations but you are not always as astute when judging the motives of close colleagues, so do consider all the options before reaching a conclusion.

You have the spirit and the energy to become an inspiring leader, but your moods and quick temper can sometimes make you unreliable. Although you have an independent streak that gives you the confidence to face challenges, you must learn to listen to the opinions and tolerate the weaknesses of others. Your talents and energy speak for themselves without you pushing yourself to the forefront, and others are likely to be attracted by your constructive ideas.

You are creative and intelligent, and once you are committed to a major project you throw yourself into it whole-heartedly, although you may well begin and then abandon many less important schemes. You have the will and the skill to realize your ideas but you can be unpredictable. In the end, the success and efficiency of a job are more important to you than the profits it may yield, although your talents will eventually provide you with financial security.

You are patient and persevering, with good powers of concentration, but if people take you for granted or interfere in your life you can be obstinate and stubborn. You are likely to have a close circle of trusted friends and do not need more than this; indeed, you often prefer the freedom of being alone. You do not feel threatened by new situations, and as long as you are not forced into anything, you are willing to leave the safety of a familiar place to explore new ground.

You have a happy and reliable nature but you can also be naive; do not naturally assume that you can trust everyone. You do not usually mull over small matters or minor insults and are quick to forgive others when you have been offended, but you should learn not to indulge people who exploit your good nature. Fortunately many honest people are drawn to you, and they provide a close-knit and protective circle.

Your perseverance and determination enable you to see projects through. But when faced with problems, you rarely seek advice as you dislike others criticizing your approach. You have a strong moral code, quickly distinguishing right from wrong, and in the face of an injustice you will not relax until the truth has been established. Although you work hard towards your goals, your efforts may not always be recognized at the time. Others, however, soon realize the work that you have put in.

You approach life intelligently and patiently and are not easily sidetracked from your goals. Once you have set your mind on something you will complete it thoroughly, although you do need to be in charge of your own life and find it hard to accept orders. Your determination and commitment to projects give you the confidence to express your opinions clearly and, if necessary, forcefully, though from time to time you need to take care not to upset others in the process.

You are kind-hearted and enthusiastic but can be too headstrong, even though you are well-intentioned. You pursue interests whole-heartedly, but your naivety and inexperience sometimes work against you, and you can be left feeling disappointed that you have not achieved your goals. You hope for the best and work to this end, so when a project flops it is hard for you to deal with the failure. Do not blame yourself when this happens, as you will often have given it your best effort.

It is hard for you to decide what really suits you. Sometimes you need company, while at other times you long for a peaceful life; sometimes you appear stubborn and at other times relaxed. You combine an extrovert and an introvert nature, but at heart you are unsure of yourself and appreciate support and reassurance. Your unpredictability can be misunderstood and you may unintentionally drive others away by appearing uninterested; try to be more confident so others realize you do care.

You appear to take life calmly and deal with events gently, but when you find yourself in unexpected or confrontational situations a more stubborn and determined streak emerges. You want to perform to the best of your abilities but are easily aggravated by interruptions or criticisms. You may find that in your professional life you have to be more accommodating and constructive in order to help others as well as yourself.

Your openness and willingness to participate enable you to develop a wide circle of friends, and you are a welcome addition to any social gathering. You put the same effort into your social life as you do into your career, and your communication skills are highly valued. However, underneath your demonstrative and attractive character lies a much more private and thoughtful person, and only those close to you see this deeper side of your nature.

Others are drawn by your sincerity and kindness, and your intuitive understanding of human nature serves you well in both your professional and personal life. Once your interest is stimulated you are a steady and enthusiastic worker, but, if anything, you are too forgiving, and your inability to make hard decisions does create unnecessary dilemmas. You do not want to offend others, but at times you should declare your opinions in order to avoid misunderstandings.

You are honest and accommodating – more likely to acquiesce and keep the peace than to argue over minor matters. But when it comes to important issues you set high standards for yourself and for others, and your confidence in your own abilities means that you will only undertake work that you know you will complete. You are able to target your efforts yet at the same time handle tensions that may arise among colleagues.

You are a talented and strong-willed leader who is driven by a firm sense of justice. You are likely to rise to projects that challenge your organizational capacities, and are ready to channel your considerable energies in defence of those who are unfairly treated. When you do make mistakes, however, you are often too critical of yourself. Failure can leave you feeling upset for a long time, so try not to dwell on your mistakes – just put them down to experience and move on.

You have an attractive combination of sincerity and good humor, which enables you to make friends easily. You set yourself high standards in your social and professional life and are easily hurt when you are the target of gossip or criticism. You feel it is important that friends and colleagues are treated with the same respect that you would expect to receive yourself, and you are unlikely to judge others hastily or reach conclusions without taking every angle into account.

Tiger

You have a straightforward and open approach to life and are not easily fooled by flattery. You are also full of hope and enthusiasm, although this can sometimes prevent you from acknowledging limitations or practicalities; you need to learn to deal with projects step by step and put time aside for forward planning. You will need to establish a firm reputation in your career before you take any risks.

You are sensitive to what is going on around you, and when friends request help you rarely refuse. You have an ability to assess issues cautiously and suggest the most appropriate course of action. You are also a reliable worker, quick to react to sudden demands and with an intelligent vision for what is required in the workplace. You also apply these energies to your social life and have a good sense of time and place, usually finding the right word for the right occasion.

②

You have an amenable and sociable nature, which encourages a wide circle of friends and colleagues. Your approach to work is serious and efficient and you are usually calm in a crisis, which enables you to assess and analyze situations competently and act accordingly. However, one of your weaknesses is your inability to keep to a schedule because you fill your time with so many activities and commitments; try not to overstretch yourself – be realistic about what you can achieve.

④

The fourth month of the tiger is considered to be one of the luckiest months of this year. You have an intelligent and hardworking nature and a talent for resolving problems. Although you enjoy working as part of a team, your talents really come to the fore when you are in control of your own career. You have a liberal approach to life and are open to most situations, and you tend to demand high standards in both your working and your romantic life.

You are good-natured and quick-witted but also have a stubborn side. You put your intelligence to good use in your career, although your determination to succeed can result in mistakes, as you often overlook well-intentioned advice. Your confidence and optimism carry you forwards but also create disappointments for yourself and for others when you fail. You are certainly capable of achieving your goals but need to be more patient and objective in your methods.

It seems that good luck is on your side in your family life and also in your career. Just when you need extra income or support, something or someone turns up to help you out and so you prosper without having to work too hard. But do not take this good fortune for granted – plan your finances carefully so you have a small income for future years. Although there may be many opportunities for romance in your life, you are likely to make a long-term commitment fairly early on.

You have a hard-working approach to life, and even when you are worn out by the demands of the day you rarely give in or admit exhaustion. If something needs to be completed, you will persevere until it is finished, and your determination will eventually be rewarded. You are sensitive to the world around you and to the suffering of others, and will make an effort not to offend or hurt those who need your help.

You have an outgoing and talkative nature and can adapt well to most social situations, but there is also a serious and thoughtful side to your character that likes independence and needs privacy. You are quick to discover if someone is trying to control you or depend on you unnecessarily, and you will soon make a hasty escape from the situation. Sometimes, however, you will need to compromise your independence so that you can spend time listening to others.

You have a liberal outlook on life and find it hard to live by conservative values. You are an active and diligent worker who rarely disturbs others to ask them for help. Although you are full of energy and will rise to the challenge of hard work, you sometimes fail to notice small but important details; make sure you give yourself more time to consider these potential pitfalls.

You approach life with a great deal of enthusiasm and often act on impulse. Even though you do not always consider the consequences of your actions, good fortune seems to be on your side and you usually manage to escape trouble. You apply admirable commitment and effort to your work, which is why you take immediate action to regain your losses if you feel that you have been deceived or cheated in any way.

You are full of energy and need the stimulation of physically active work or hobbies. You also have an impatient streak and want everything to happen and finish quickly so that you can go on to pursue your next interest. Even if you suffer a setback along the way, you push it aside and look to the future, driven on by an optimism that rarely leaves you the time to mull over the disappointments of the past.

You have a confident and generous nature, and in many instances you forgive those who have hurt you. Your ability to believe in what you do, combined with a firm but calm approach, make you a good negotiator. You do not like to be caught up in trivial affairs, and when it comes to money you rarely argue over minor financial matters; as the Chinese say, "A big chicken never pecks small rice."

Rabbit

You have a positive attitude to life but also tread cautiously and sensibly, avoiding publicity or stressful situations. If you are put under pressure, you become increasingly tense, but there is no need to rush because your intelligence and intuition should help you to succeed at your own pace. Your elegant and skilful approach to life inspires others, and even though you do not actively seek attention you will build up a following of dedicated friends.

You have a forgiving, caring nature and know how to put people at ease. You are also a good listener, and many people confide in you knowing that their thoughts and secrets are safe. Although you are cautious and carefully check details before you make commitments, when you do make up your mind you act swiftly and without hesitation. You are a skilled independent worker but are soon unsettled when unexpected problems arise, so give yourself time and space to consider the best course of action.

You do not like to interfere in other people's lives, preferring instead to focus on your own business and affairs. However, this detachment creates a single-mindedness that may prevent you from spotting interesting opportunities or widening your circle of friends, so try to be more open in your approach. You do, nevertheless, have an enthusiastic outlook on life and your kindness and tranquillity are appreciated.

You approach tasks methodically and carefully, making sure that you pay attention to small details. You are a perfectionist but you also change your mind often, which inevitably affects your ability to make a final decision or finish a job according to its original plan. Although you are able to recognize your mistakes, you need the support and encouragement of trusted friends to publicly acknowledge or discuss them.

You are well-respected for your wisdom, courage and energy and treat others with the same consideration that you would expect to receive yourself. You have a strong sense of morality, which you apply in all your affairs, but be careful not to make hasty decisions. When you fail, you often lose the confidence to try again instead of learning from your mistakes; do not lose heart, as fresh opportunities will come your way – and you will most likely be aware of the possible pitfalls, too.

You have an enthusiastic and lively approach to life but often lack the confidence to go in search of fresh opportunities. You have a patient and discreet nature, but you need to learn to be more strong-willed in competitive situations. Once you find a secure environment, however, you will be more willing to adapt to change and will feel sufficiently comfortable to handle responsibility, deal with challenges and develop your ideas.

Your openness and dependability are appreciated by friends, who know that you can be relied upon to be reasonable in difficult circumstances. You are easily disturbed or startled by other people's arguments or outbursts of anger, and there are times when you need to be more courageous. Sometimes your unwillingness to face up to hostile situations will land you in even more complex ones, but you are intuitive enough to eventually find a means of escape.

You are intelligent, forgiving and courageous, but in your eagerness to organize you often make hasty and rash decisions and act without careful consideration. In the end, you are aware of your faults and find it easy to forgive other people for their mistakes, but nevertheless you should try to plan ahead to complete your work more efficiently. You are observant and interested in the world around you, and are particularly attracted by modern ideas and new technology.

You have a deep empathy for the problems and heartache of others but find it hard to express your own emotions. Sometimes you feel it is inappropriate to make suggestions, while at other times your anxiety obscures your true feelings. Although you can appear to be difficult or obstinate, inwardly you are gentle and accommodating; it just takes a little time for friends to perceive your sensitivity.

You are romantic, nostalgic and emotional but sometimes carried away by enthusiasm. You can overwhelm new acquaintances in your eagerness to understand them, but despite this you do have a natural talent for creating a good ambience. You have a strong empathy for the suffering of others and are soon won over to sympathetic causes. Your solid sense of morality engenders generosity but can also make you critical of approaches different to your own, so try not to make rash judgements.

You are sensitive to the emotions and needs of others, and it is unlikely that you will be taken advantage of since you are a good judge of character. Those who come to you asking for help are treated with dignity, understanding and patience, and in return they know you will treat their disclosures with confidence. You rarely entrust your own secrets to others, however, and sometimes suffer in silence when you could easily be offered reassurance if you shared your worries.

You are cool and collected, gifted with a good memory and an analytical mind. However, you do not like others curtailing your independence and are wary of new acquaintances or unfamiliar suggestions. Sometimes you form opinions without hearing all the facts, but this is simply your way of trying to protect yourself, as beneath your tough, cool exterior you are easily hurt by the words and deeds of others. Thus, there are times when you need to develop a more critical, resilient front.

Dragon

You are talented and hard-working, with strong reserves of patience and energy. If you are presented with two tasks you will apply the same dedication to both and are capable of completing them to the expected standard. Your resolution to succeed in satisfying both yourself and others is expressed in your private life as well as in your professional life. This is combined with a direct approach that enables you to express your emotions and opinions honestly and confidently.

2

Sometimes you create the impression of being shy or weak, but those who know you recognize your confidence and bravery. You are not afraid to accept a challenge, but it is important that you feel stimulated by your work. When you are dedicated to a project, nothing will stand in your way, though dissatisfaction may creep in when tasks become mundane or repetitive. You have great hopes and dreams in your life, but do plan carefully before you act.

You manage to combine gentleness with determination, which makes you a trusted and inspiring leader. You are alert and responsive to all manner of issues and have the confidence not only to make decisions but also to carry them through to their conclusion. Although you can be stern when the need arises, you also have an appealing and well-intentioned nature that is valued by your friends and your family.

4

You are brimming with energy and confidence, and when inspired by an issue or a cause, you believe in it passionately; setbacks or the prospect of failure will not deter you from completing what you set out to do. You are intelligent and usually sufficiently alert to identify problems before they are blown out of proportion. Your awareness of your talents can make you over-confident, although your understanding and protectiveness mean your weaknesses are soon forgiven.

Your determination to fight for just causes or to resolve disputes is both recognized and respected. Many are impressed by your tenacity and have high expectations of you – and they are rarely disappointed. However, your occasional shyness sometimes masks your courage and optimism and makes it hard for you to form immediate friendships, although those close to you value your considerate nature, and in time colleagues and acquaintances will also recognize your strength and kindness.

You have remarkable energy and determination and will go to great lengths to achieve your goals. You tend to thrive on challenges and are able to flourish in a competitive world where your negotiation techniques and adept planning can be used to full effect. You are likely to have many skills and are a dedicated worker, but you need to feel that your talents are recognized and admired; when your skills are appreciated it gives you an extra boost to rise to complex challenges.

Your quick wit and adaptability will soon inspire confidence among friends and colleagues. You are not afraid to tackle problems or accept complex tasks, and once your attention is focused on your work you are rarely distracted. There is a gentle and caring side to your character, but when you are in a competitive environment a more aggressive and dominant side emerges, and you apply yourself to tasks with much enthusiasm and determination.

This is the most creative month of the dragon year and your mind is likely to be buzzing with new ideas. You have a talent for expressing these ideas and for spotting interesting angles or opportunities in everyday situations. You prefer to use your own intuition when you are involved in a project and rarely trouble others with unnecessary questions. Although you are courageous and energetic, do be careful that your enthusiasm is not undermined by a lack of research.

You have a sharp intellect and abundant energy and self-confidence. You are ready to volunteer help when someone needs an organizer or leader, and your sound judgement is appreciated. You are full of practical ideas, and it is unlikely you will ever be short of money, although you may need to curb an extravagant streak. You should also beware of taking risks on investments that promise high returns; they may sound tempting, but take time to consider all the financial possibilities.

Your mind is packed full of projects and ideas, and you have both the determination and the talent to see them through. You have an honest and trusting nature but you should stop to consider the drawbacks before you commit yourself to a task. You involve yourself fully with people or situations but sometimes you are too emotional, and when this happens you should hold back and seek objective advice.

You have many talents and ideas but sometimes you are too sensitive or conservative to express them. Do not underestimate your capabilities, since you are an able and skilled worker. You can be overwhelmed easily by boisterous company, and when you are suddenly confronted by the unknown you may lose confidence. However, once you have become accustomed to people and situations you have the potential to be both astute and organized in your dealings.

You can be very accommodating and cheerful, but when you are in a competitive situation a more determined and ambitious side of your nature appears. You are not easily distracted from your goals but you need to be careful not to rush into an agreement without adequate forethought. You are often helped by unexpected good fortune, but beware of missing these lucky opportunities through being too single-minded – try to be more open to the events and ideas around you.

Snake

You have an active, questioning mind, ready to explore new possibilities and gain new information. Indeed, you are sometimes too inquisitive of other people's secrets and can rarely keep what you find to yourself. You are well-liked and have many friends because of your amenable approach to life, but you may miss out on career opportunities as you are not forceful enough. You will be more successful if you have faith in yourself and ignore the critical comments of others.

You have an unpredictable side to your character: sometimes you are open and energetic, at other times cool and reserved. This can confuse and disorientate those who know you, leaving them uncertain of how they stand. If you are in the same company for too long or working on a lengthy project, you tend to become impatient or dissatisfied as your initial enthusiasm wears away. Try to concentrate on working on one scheme at a time to make sure that your goals are accomplished.

To the outside world you appear lively and confident, but there is a suspicious side to your character that makes you doubt the motives of others. You do not easily accept orders or take on new ideas as you feel insecure of your own skills; you do not enjoy quarrelling but simply lack confidence. You are suited, therefore, to careers or interests that give you the freedom to plan your life on your own terms and pursue your own interests, especially ones based on study and research.

You approach life seriously and have the skill and determination to succeed in your career – but do not assume that everyone will work at your pace or follow your methods. Try to be more understanding of your colleagues' weaknesses and more appreciative of their strengths. Your seriousness may put others off, so you need to be more relaxed and informal. At times you also assume others share your idealism, but remember they may not have the energy or commitment to match your own.

One of your greatest strengths is your sense of justice, and when you feel someone has been unfairly treated you usually rise to their defence. But you also have a stubborn and critical streak, and although you can be tolerant you are determined to operate on your own terms, often imposing your standards on those you help. You are well-intentioned but your stubbornness can make you seem insensitive, so try to let others express their opinions and have a role in decision-making.

You have an intelligent and alert nature; you know how to put your skills to good use and make them work to your advantage. When you are faced with a dilemma, you can assess the situation quickly, and your sharp intuition enables you to act accordingly. You know how to focus your energies at work but you also know how to enjoy life's pleasures, with many people attracted by your open, cheerful and perceptive nature.

You are dependable and hard-working and have a natural ability to relate to a wide variety of people. You do, however, need independence and can be hesitant about acting on advice if it limits your freedom. Your opinions change frequently and you can seem inconstant and flighty, although you are in fact serious and alert. Your romantic life is likely to be active, but you often treat romance as a game and it may take time for you to settle down.

You have a great enthusiasm for life and adapt easily to different people and situations. You are thoughtful, amenable and good fun, and when you need companionship your friends will always be there. Your sharp judgement and quick reactions make you a natural leader, but you can be inconsistent, which denies you access to some profitable opportunities. When interested in a project, you show a great deal of imagination, but do give yourself a chance to identify possibilities in less inspiring situations.

You are a determined worker and once you have established your targets you are unlikely to be distracted. You know how to focus your attention and will persevere until the task is finished, regardless of any obstacles in your way. You are irritated by unnecessary distractions, but more diplomacy may be needed in both your professional and personal lives in order to keep the peace with those around you.

Your honesty and judgement inspire trust, and your willingness to adapt to most situations makes you well-respected. Although you are an active and intelligent worker, you also have an impulsive streak, which you are aware needs to be controlled. Every now and then a careless side to your nature also emerges when you do not have the energy or the inclination to meet immediate demands. Others, however, may be relying on you, and that extra effort will be appreciated.

You are intelligent but sometimes lack the confidence needed to take on responsibilities. You are trusting and kind, although this can be a flaw if you allow yourself to be too gullible, since you are easily upset when you feel that others have taken advantage of you personally or professionally. If you set yourself reasonable targets, you have the wisdom to achieve them, but do take each stage one step at a time.

You are generous, just and open and have the determination to persevere until you achieve your goals. You are good company but find it hard to accept advice or listen to opinions that contrast with your own, and before long you believe it is your duty to express what you feel. When you do disagree with someone, you are a straightforward speaker, although diplomacy might serve you better in sensitive situations.

Horse

You have a striking presence, which naturally draws attention. Your intelligence and patience enable you to persevere, regardless of setbacks, but your determination can also bring out a self-centered streak that makes you resilient to offers of support or advice. You also have a reserved side to your nature and occasionally withdraw into your shell, thereby missing valuable opportunities. However, you just need some extra encouragement from those close to you to rebuild your confidence.

You have a kind and generous nature, but your daydreaming can distract you from reality. Your hopes and ambitions may often be pitched too high, ultimately resulting in disappointment, so you are tempted to ease this with thoughts of new adventures or challenges. You do, however, have a courageous character that wins respect, but do not exhaust your energies trying too hard to prove yourself since others will already be aware of your capabilities and efforts.

You have a strong and generous character and a keen interest in people and events. Your concern for others and your willingness to fight for just causes makes you impassioned, but be careful not to be naive; sometimes your strong beliefs prevent you from seeing the ways of the world. Although you have natural charm, which quickly attracts attention, do not assume that you will automatically be the center of attention or you may be disappointed.

You have an active nature and you organize your life carefully, but your determination to have everything run according to plan may irritate others. People do appreciate the care you take over matters and the style with which you carry out your work, but your obstinacy may undermine your efforts. If family and friends offer you advice, try to consider what they say, rather than rejecting it in favor of your own decisions.

You have creative talent and know how to channel your energy into a specific task, particularly if it is something that you find stimulating. You also have a good understanding of other people and take time to appreciate their motives and emotions. Your ability to see and interpret what is happening around you should help you to gauge your actions accordingly, although you are sometimes carried away by excitement or enthusiasm so try to keep this in check when you can.

You have an honest and outgoing approach to life, which makes you suited to a career as a diplomat, entrepreneur or politician. You are not afraid to express what you feel, but you also have the intelligence to express your opinions according to your audience. You have a brave nature and pursue the truth with passionate belief, a passion that is also particularly evident in your romantic life.

You are thoughtful and honorable, handling your family and your career with care. You take time to understand what others are thinking or feeling and have a strong empathy for their sorrows and problems. This willingness to consider others is appreciated, but by doing so you sometimes fail to see good opportunities in your own life. Put some time aside for yourself so you can analyze the possibilities around you and respond to them constructively.

You are swept along by your emotions and your enthusiasm, and in this charged state you sometimes fail to consider the practicalities of your actions. Once you have devised a plan, you rush ahead to put it into effect, and while this energy is impressive you must be careful not to offend or ignore others in the process. Try to calm your swift changes of mood so that you have time to consider what lies ahead.

You have a straightforward, honest and open character and are uncomplicated in your emotions. You are sensitive to criticism and easily hurt by careless actions, and have a natural empathy for others who may be offended or suffering in some way. You are unlikely to refuse requests for help but rarely ask others for favors. Relationships with your family and friends are trusting and strong, and though your reliability may make you appear unadventurous you are intelligent and perceptive.

You are confident and intelligent, inspired by people, conversations or circumstances that others might take for granted. This creative ability makes you a good researcher or inventor. You are courageous and self-reliant, and can let pride stand in your way when you need to seek advice. You do not want others to assume you have carried out your work inefficiently or that you have any weaknesses, but more than likely they will be flattered if you ask their opinion.

You have a strong independent streak and pursue your personal goals, confident of your own skills. You are optimistic and imaginative but you also take the time to listen to a variety of opinions and consider the effects of your actions. You like to deal with incidents in your own time and do not always work at the pace that others may expect. Sometimes your methods are unconventional, but you have your own particular style and this usually produces the required result.

You are thoughtful towards family and friends and are an intelligent judge of character, although there may be times when you prefer not to face the reality of a situation. Your moods can be unpredictable: sometimes you seem selfish, at other times generous; one minute you seek solitude, the next you throw yourself into a busy social life. Generally people accept these sudden mood swings, but on occasion you will need to establish a careful balance to deal effectively with your situation.

Ram

You have an independent nature, confident enough to try something new instead of following the crowd. You are also truthful and, aware of the injustices you see around you, you are not afraid to speak out. This is helped by the fact that you are a strong and emotive speaker, but be careful not to overestimate your own ability. You are a popular character and others are willing to support you; when they do offer you advice, learn to trust them.

You have a natural empathy for others and will usually offer whatever help you can – and your kindness is not forgotten. You are not an ambitious person and are content to lead a peaceful life, but unexpected opportunities will come your way that allow you to step into the limelight. Be cautious in business and plan according to your ability and the finances available, and you should find that you reap the benefits in the future.

You are hard-working but reserved, and when you have innovative ideas you are wary of putting them forward, preferring others to take the initiative. You also have an independent streak, and while you do not mind being guided you dislike taking direct orders. This makes you best suited to a job such as a researcher or one where another person sets the framework but you are allowed to work at your own pace.

You are a thoughtful and solitary person who sometimes appears aloof, but this is only because you find it hard to express your feelings. It takes time for you to respond to gestures of friendship or requests for help. You can also be obstinate, and if you do not think a job is worth finishing you will turn your mind elsewhere. However, to inspire confidence you may find that you need to persevere more.

You are talkative and elegant, and these characteristics enable you to adapt well to different environments. You are sensitive to what you see and hear and are careful how you present yourself, but you are also wary of taking responsibility or of making decisions that will affect others. You have an impatient streak and are tempted to abandon projects when difficulties arise; with a little more patience you will be able to find a solution to these problems.

You are kind and thoughtful, with a natural ability to make others feel welcome in your company and at ease in their conversation. This is a particularly lucky month for the ram since it forecasts a peaceful and happy life. Your best advice is to make the most of this natural good fortune, but do not take it for granted – if dissatisfaction creeps in, this auspiciousness could change to misfortune, so take care.

You have a kind and honest nature; you take life in your stride and rarely worry about day-to-day matters. You naturally develop a strong level of trust with your friends, and it is rare for you ever to let them down. You also have a strong sense of justice, and if you find yourself in a position of authority or influence you are likely to use it wisely. All in all, you are a popular friend whose openness and honesty are greatly appreciated.

You have a natural ability to adapt to people and places, and are quick to react when others need you. Your concentration and attention to detail will serve you well in your career, although you should be careful not to be too stubborn if things are not going in your favor. Learn to accept advice and act on it. It may be hard to find work that suits you when you are young, but do not give up hope since career opportunities will improve over the years.

You are a perfectionist and expect the same standards from your friends and family as you expect from yourself. You are capable and trustworthy but you tend to take life too seriously – do not be upset when others fail to act or think in the way you want. Try to be more relaxed and concentrate on the present rather than the future, since your eagerness to strive ahead may distract you from the enjoyment of your life as you live it.

You have a reserved nature and assess situations calmly; it is rare for you to be carried away by extreme emotions. You are also determined to achieve your goals and can be jealous when others are successful, feeling that your efforts are not fully recognized. Your intelligence and ambition should be enough to create the openings you need, and relationships with your colleagues will be more likely to prosper when you support their successes.

You have an alert nature, aware of the details and complexities of situations, and are a good judge of character, able to assess people intelligently. When called on to speak, you can express yourself eloquently, and you are not short of friends or admirers. However, your impatience and frequent changes of mind are weaknesses that may create difficulties when you are trying to build long-term relationships; more patience and stability will help to establish strong foundations.

You have a just and idealistic side to your character, mindful of the needs of others and willing to campaign for them. Essentially you have a kind nature, but your manner is brusque and sometimes so straightforward that you can sound abrupt, so try to choose your words carefully. You are, however, sensitive to what is happening around you, and when trouble is brewing you try in your own way to resolve the situation.

Monkey

You are an organized and skilled planner, paying attention to the minor details that others may ignore, yet at the same time you have a vision for the overall scheme of your work. In your enthusiasm and determination to complete projects efficiently to the agreed deadline, you may overlook the actions and advice of others, so from time to time stop and ask their opinions. Thus there will be times when you need to handle affairs more cautiously in your career – and also in romance.

2

You have the intelligence and the commitment to achieve your goals, but sometimes you are too sensitive to criticisms and become unnecessarily sidetracked. You can generally assess situations and characters well and you are honest with your opinions, but at times you place too much trust in colleagues and are disappointed when they fail to live up to your expectations. Try not to overestimate the amount of support they are able to give you.

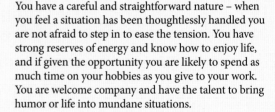

You have a careful and straightforward nature – when you feel a situation has been thoughtlessly handled you are not afraid to step in to ease the tension. You have strong reserves of energy and know how to enjoy life, and if given the opportunity you are likely to spend as much time on your hobbies as you give to your work. You are welcome company and have the talent to bring humor or life into mundane situations.

You have a lively imagination and a strong moral code, confident enough to speak out when asked to do something that goes against your principles. When you focus on an issue that interests you, you work diligently to achieve what you want, and when it is completed you are likely to go off in search of a new challenge. You are good at identifying opportunities or finding quick routes through complex matters, and so you would make a skilled entrepreneur.

You have an intelligent understanding of what is happening around you and are quick to react to the unexpected. You are ready to fight for worthy causes and are not afraid of competition or confrontation, but you would rather resolve arguments than create them. There is a more carefree side to your character, though; in social company your entertaining skills soon become apparent, and before long you forget about life's worries.

You have an observant and charismatic character that quickly draws people into your world. You are at ease in a wide variety of circumstances, where you can assess the mood and interests of those around you and then deftly apply your conversational skills. From time to time, however, you are distracted by minor or trivial matters and lose touch with the more important issues, so you need to try to keep your attention focused on immediate matters.

You have a confident and just nature and are rarely overwhelmed by crises or defeated by difficulties. You are elegant in movement and appearance as well as careful in speech, finding appropriate and subtle ways of stating your opinion. Challenges and new opportunities quickly attract your interest, and when you are committed to a cause you fight with energy and determination, and are unlikely to deviate until you have met your goals.

You are straightforward and determined, sometimes to the point of stubbornness, so you perhaps need to be more malleable in your reactions and attitudes. There is, however, a more accommodating and relaxed side to your nature, and you are open to important requests for help, although you are also a stern judge and rarely waste your time on frivolous issues. You are likely to have a strong creative streak, which is expressed in your interests and in eloquent conversation.

You are sensitive to the world around you, and sometimes you interpret incidental actions or words too seriously. You need to recognize your talents – you have determination and courage, though you lack self-confidence. At times you are overcome by doubts and consequently feel you have to push yourself hard to prove that you are capable. In fact, you can be perceptive and astute, and just need to focus your energies rather than allow yourself to be distracted.

Your alert and active nature flourishes in lively, stimulating environments. You take care of your appearance and mind your manners, and, when the situation demands, you are an accomplished speaker. All in all, you create a positive, reassuring impression. However, the thought of being isolated or confined to one space makes you restless, and your creative energy is drained when you are limited by a routine. Thus your job needs to allow flexibility but also involve contact with others.

You combine openness and generosity with a passion for life, and you enthusiastically pursue new interests. You have an unconventional character and an unusual approach to work but fulfill your commitments nevertheless. You find subtle ways to avoid confrontation and enjoy relating to others, although this may distract you from immediate tasks. From time to time your imagination wanders as you dream about new ideas; do try not to lose touch with reality in the process.

You create a steady balance in your life between professional and personal commitments. You are generous with your time and even-handed in your approach, but at the same time you are a determined worker – all qualities that inspire trust among friends and colleagues. You have the determination to see a project through to its conclusion, and while you pay attention to detail you are not preoccupied by minor matters or trivial mistakes.

Rooster

You are brave and outgoing, not easily intimidated by influential company or unexpected situations. You actually enjoy the challenge of meeting new people or being caught up in controversial issues, and would therefore make a good politician or diplomat. When tact is required, you can rise to the occasion and efficiently handle delicate matters. You enjoy life but are tempted to overindulge, so try to keep a healthy balance in your life overall.

You present a cool, confident front in public and as a result can appear selfish or proud. In fact, you are a good observer and an alert judge of situations, and are quick to react if you sense an injustice. You are sensitive and courageous and have a strong sense of direction; you usually know how far to push an issue and when to withdraw. Although you are open and approachable, there is also a possessive side to your character, and you form strong attachments to friends and family.

You do not like to be deprived of your independence and react quickly if you feel your freedom is being compromised, especially if someone in a position of influence is trying to advise or control you. You have an intelligent outlook on life and your individuality is admired. However, you are also headstrong, and in times of trouble you should relent and take advice from friends – the support they offer could help you out of sensitive situations.

You have an enquiring mind and are not afraid to ask questions or withdraw from situations that may make others uncomfortable. You combine this inquisitiveness with an open and tolerant attitude, and when you find that someone needs your help you can be a generous friend. Although you have many strong social skills, you sometimes probe into areas that would be better left alone and thereby unintentionally upset others, so try to be more cautious when broaching a sensitive topic.

You are a good judge of character and have an energetic and straightforward approach to life. You are generally astute in assessing situations and can soon determine if someone is trying to take advantage of you. You are quick to analyze and react, which makes you a competent leader, though you also have a proud and independent streak, which may undermine your authority. Give yourself and others time to discuss problems so that complex matters can be resolved.

You are sensitive to what is going on around you and easily upset by disturbances in your life. You start projects enthusiastically and are eager to finish work, but you lack the patience that is needed and often turn to others to help you to pick up the pieces. Try to concentrate more on the present so that you can focus your attention on relevant details. As others come to understand you, they will find that although you appear to be hasty, you do have a more capable, determined side.

You are drawn to new developments and ideas and have a talent for organizing material methodically. When you accept work or pursue a new interest, you sift through the relevant information and cast off anything superfluous. Although you channel your attention well, do not abandon hope when some projects inevitably fail, since there will be a chance to revive them afresh. You approach new friendships cautiously, but when you do form a relationship you are generous and committed.

You relish life and the opportunities that lie ahead and know how to make the most of them. However, you are often so busy pursuing your own interests that you forget the promises you have made or else are sidetracked by other matters. You are full of enthusiasm but need to direct your energies towards immediate responsibilities. You like to create a good impression through your style and appearance, and you are likely to have a strong interest in color and design, reflecting your creative side.

You enjoy personal contact and can be emotional and courageous, impatient and charismatic. You are stimulated by the world around you and express your individuality in your ideas, actions and appearance. You thrive in situations where you are given freedom and can be easily frustrated if you feel trapped or controlled. You need the companionship of others and tend to become bored or depressed when you spend too much time alone; plan your diary so that you have regular company.

You are a strong leader and a determined fighter, but although you appear to have strong reserves of energy you are emotionally and physically sensitive to your environment. In your efforts to succeed you can be proud or obstinate, but those who know you well recognize a more gentle and understanding side of your character and grow to trust and admire you because of it. When others are in trouble, you are a good listener and a supportive friend.

You have a natural innocence and are both startled and stimulated by the world around you. It is easy for others to exploit your naivety, although many will be attracted to you and helpful precisely because of your innocent charm. You are a skilled debater and enjoy investigating problems and finding solutions, and despite the fact that you set yourself difficult challenges you work with great determination to achieve them.

You are open to opinions and have a just, emotive and generous nature. You are impassioned in your beliefs and persuasive in your arguments, so when challenged you will steadfastly defend your standpoint. You are rarely sidetracked from your aims and usually pursue your goals fearlessly and steadily, normally working on your own since you need peace and privacy to concentrate. When you believe in an issue, you will defend others with as much enthusiasm as you would defend yourself.

Dog

You are a peaceful and steady worker whose attention is clearly focused, right up until a task is finished. You hate to leave anything incomplete, but this single-mindedness also brings out a stubborn streak that might obscure the overall aims of your work. You are honest in your approach to life, caring towards friends and most of the time at peace with the world. You also have a sharp mind and can easily clarify and deal with problems.

You are a good judge of character, quick to react to situations or defend others. Your energy is admirable and you have many talents, but you must be careful that your good intentions are not misunderstood; you are not always able to express yourself as diplomatically or as eloquently as you would like, and criticism does hurt your sensitive nature. Despite your lack of eloquence, you have good taste and a creative streak that is suited to an artistic career.

You are brave and hard-working, and when you feel secure you are not afraid to rise to challenges. You are an astute judge of character and are open to a variety of points of view. Always ready to fight for good causes, you are particularly moved if you feel that someone has been unfairly treated; you will be only too willing to sacrifice some of your own time or money for the cause.

You have strong resources of energy and will usually take on the most complex tasks. Determination, honesty and good sense are your strengths, but at times you try too hard to impress. However, your accommodating nature compensates for this and you are welcome in almost any social situation. You care what others think, but avoid reading too much into their conversations or actions since you can be over-emotional and may upset yourself unnecessarily.

You are quick-witted, with a vivid imagination. You are also honest in your personal relationships and sensitive to the world around you – sometimes too sensitive. When you hear of other people's troubles you empathize with them to the extent that you often upset yourself. In order to cope more efficiently, you will have to come to terms with life's hardships, although your sympathetic approach provides you with a supportive family and circle of friends.

You are courageous, intelligent and strong, and when you see a problem appear on the horizon you are quick to react. Your robust nature means you rarely suffer health problems. You have the potential to be a skilful leader but you dislike taking orders, especially from those you consider to be intellectually inferior to you. You are alert to the needs of others and are happy to sort out their problems; in return, other people are usually at your side when you need help.

You have a generous nature and take a liberal and optimistic approach to life. Your readiness to give your time to others makes you well-liked, but you also have a proud streak. You refuse to let obstacles stand in your way and are able to find ingenious ways of meeting your goals. While this tough attitude will help you to achieve success, be careful not to alienate others; you may disturb established routines or plans without realizing. So, when confronted by an obstacle, exercise caution.

Your strengths are your adaptability and perseverance, and even in the most unlikely circumstances you will manage to find your own niche. You are willing to accept responsibility, and although others may see you as weak you have unexpected reserves of strength. You know when you have made a mistake and you have the courage to correct it, but in doing so your temper is sometimes pushed to the limit; at times such as this, hold back, before you say something you regret.

You can assess situations quickly but need time to react and are wary of those who are more decisive than you. You need peace and quiet in which to reflect or plan, so avoid agreeing to work to tight deadlines. Do not be too ambitious and, even when under pressure, give yourself space to assess problems step by step and your efforts will be rewarded. You have a gentle, thoughtful nature and do not want to make demands on – or control – others, so you are best suited to working within a hierarchy.

Your active approach to life, combined with a generous outlook, will attract a wide variety of friends, who offer you the support you need when faced by a crisis. You do not like confrontation, and when you are faced by pressure you tend to slip into an imaginary world to avoid any conflict. In order to deal with the problems life throws at you, try to focus your energy and concentration when the first signs of trouble appear.

You are confident among colleagues and friends and happy to step forwards to take control. You know how to focus on the important issues, but your determined approach sometimes becomes the target of criticism. What few people glimpse is the reserved and thoughtful side of your nature. Your many natural talents may induce jealousy in others, which will eventually affect your social and professional life, so do make an effort to befriend those who initially appear hostile.

You are hard-working and attentive, but you also have a competitive streak that sometimes spills over into your social life. In your efforts to achieve your aims, you may unwittingly hurt others, so try to gauge the effect your actions may have. You are watchful of those around you and respond cautiously to sudden requests, but if someone really needs your help you can be courageous. At heart, you are considerate, but you need to be more tolerant so others can recognize your sensitive nature.

Pig

You are intelligent and sincere, with the determination to complete tasks and fulfill your promises. There is an ambitious side to your nature that emerges when your interest is stimulated, but at times your reactions are too slow to benefit from opportunities and you may have to speed up your responses and decision-making if you are not to miss out. You apply the same honesty to romance as you do to your work, and you are likely to have strong and durable relationships.

You combine honesty with good financial judgement, and this should help you to prosper in business. You form strong bonds with colleagues and friends – a talent that will serve you well in your career – but try not to become preoccupied with the idea of fortune or success. Your projects often run smoothly at the beginning and then difficulties begin to emerge, but do not abandon hope because you have the patience and determination to overcome these obstacles.

You are courageous and straightforward but often distracted from your goals. Time is spent thinking about new possibilities or the end results of a project instead of focusing on the immediate demands. Sometimes luck seems to be running against you, but in fact it is working in your favor – you just need to concentrate on current matters, put in sufficient groundwork and take each step gradually. You may suddenly be rewarded for projects that you thought had come to an end.

You have a quick wit and are naturally at ease in company. Your conversation is wide-ranging and you can adapt to light-hearted or serious issues, although you are sometimes affected by anxiety or nervousness when surrounded by unknown faces. You are true to your word, and once you have made a commitment you have the energy and the ambition to see it through to its conclusion – even if it means having to overcome your apprehension of unfamiliar issues or people.

You are a trustworthy friend and colleague, but at times you take work so seriously you fail to see what is happening around you. Fortunately, you have the patience and strength to correct these oversights and re-establish relationships that may have been overlooked. Although you can rise to challenges, your confidence needs to be nurtured – too much responsibility makes you nervous. You just need a little encouragement from others; once reassured, you can meet the demands made of you.

You need time to assess the potential and the drawbacks of a situation before you make a decision, but once you have made a commitment you are a quick and confident worker. You are sensitive, easily upset by small problems or incidental remarks, and need to be reassured that all is well. You care about others and want to help them, and are open to new suggestions and ideas. But it is important that you recognize your limitations and do not place yourself under too much pressure.

You make friends easily but sometimes you are too outspoken and regret words that have been said in haste. You are enthusiastic and want problems to be resolved or events to be organized quickly, and if friends are in trouble you make an effort to ease their difficulties as soon as possible. You recognize that you are easily bored when a project drags on too long, particularly at work, but, if circumstances demand, you do have the perseverance and patience to see the project through.

You have an open and charitable outlook on life and find it easy to make friends in the most unlikely places. You are a responsible and active leader, and once you have made a promise you will fulfill your word, regardless of the physical demands it may involve. You have a lucky streak and opportunities usually present themselves when you least expect them – so when you think there is no hope in a project, just be patient, as a second chance will often appear.

You have a sensitive and kind nature, aware of what is happening around you and ready to offer help if it is needed. You approach life seriously, paying just as much attention to the smaller details as you do to the larger issues. You are a resolute and efficient worker and, at the risk of exhausting yourself, you endeavor to meet the high expectations that others have of you. Try to recognize the warning signs of pressure and give yourself time to recover and renew your resources.

Your honesty and warmth enable you to form long-lasting and firm friendships. You are not afraid to express an opinion, but you take into consideration the circumstances and emotions of those around you to avoid unnecessary offence. You have a resolute nature, but you are also open to advice, and if you think your actions are going to have a negative effect you will find another course of action to take.

You are alert to your surroundings and have the courage to take responsibility in times of crisis. Because you are sensitive to events, you feel that you have to speak out when you see an injustice – but you can be too outspoken. Once you have formed an opinion, you will confidently stick by it and it may take some persuasion for you to change your mind. But, in the end, you will listen to constructive advice.

You have a cheerful and open nature, and although you are a capable worker you need reassurance from friends and family. You are straightforward and honest, and when you are confident in an issue or believe in a project you work with determination and courage. If anything, your commitment can make you too outspoken, so you need to be careful that you do not unwittingly offend others in your enthusiasm to defend a cause.

5 Three Lives

HOROSCOPES

This ancient Three Lives divination system was traditionally used to reveal a boy's fortune at birth, although the forecasts are equally applicable to adult males and females.

The original Three Lives book, thought to have been written by a group of wandering Buddhist and Taoist monks making a living from selling their religious and magical skills, contains nearly fifty charts and sets of readings, which not only predict *this* life but also reveal details of your *past* life and your *future* life – hence the "three" lives. The system dates back to around 1500 CE, although many of the references it contains appear in much older astrological texts.

A Three Lives reading would have been given by one of these "wild" monks, skilled in interpreting this complex system. The reading, written on red paper in black ink, would have been consulted on special occasions, such as leaving home, getting married or choosing a career.

In this chapter, various divination methods (adapted for present-day use) have been chosen from the oldest and most popular Chinese edition of the Three Lives system. These methods offer insight on personality traits, skills and your fortune from year to year.

ANIMAL BONE FORTUNE

Just as a skeleton constitutes the underlying framework for a body, the "bones" of the twelve animal signs form the underlying framework of your horoscope. Rather than involving the casting of bones, as the name suggests, these forecasts reveal your personality type according to your hour and month of birth. They give an extra dimension to the general animal sign readings.

By now you should know your lunar month of birth, but if you need to refresh your memory turn to pages 118–27. To discover the Earthly Branch for your hour of birth refer to the table on page 76. Then, find your Earthly Branch in the table below, read down the column until you find your lunar month, and read across the chart to see which forecast applies to you.

EARTHLY BRANCH FOR HOUR OF BIRTH												ANIMAL BONE
Tzu	Ch'ou	Yin	Mao	Ch'en	Szu	Wu	Wei	Shen	Yu	Hsu	Hai	
1	2	3	4	5	6	7	8	9	10	11	12	Rat
2	3	4	5	6	7	8	9	10	11	12	1	Ox
3	4	5	6	7	8	9	10	11	12	1	2	Tiger
4	5	6	7	8	9	10	11	12	1	2	3	Rabbit
5	6	7	8	9	10	11	12	1	2	3	4	Dragon
6	7	8	9	10	11	12	1	2	3	4	5	Snake
7	8	9	10	11	12	1	2	3	4	5	6	Horse
8	9	10	11	12	1	2	3	4	5	6	7	Ram
9	10	11	12	1	2	3	4	5	6	7	8	Monkey
10	11	12	1	2	3	4	5	6	7	8	9	Rooster
11	12	1	2	3	4	5	6	7	8	9	10	Dog
12	1	2	3	4	5	6	7	8	9	10	11	Pig

LUNAR MONTH OF BIRTH

RAT BONE

You like to observe and assess situations before you make a commitment, and although you fulfill your obligations you also need to know that there is a means of escape so your independence is not compromised.

OX BONE

You learn from positive and negative experiences and store this knowledge away for future use. Although you are gentle and tolerant, there comes a point at which you feel it is necessary to object, and you can be a stubborn and determined opponent.

TIGER BONE

You are determined and inventive enough to develop your own ideas, and so would make a good entrepreneur. When you believe in an idea, you will be subtly persuasive and will steadily persevere until others are also convinced.

RABBIT BONE

At heart you are looking for a peaceful and harmonious environment that gives you the security to pursue new ideas enthusiastically. However, your attention often wanders, so you will need to make an extra effort to remain focused if work is not to be left unfinished.

DRAGON BONE

You are elegant, charming and relaxed company. Although you are not afraid of challenge or debate, you cleverly manoeuvre the conversation to avoid confrontation, a skill that will serve you well in your career.

SNAKE BONE

You are interested in color, design, your environment and your appearance. You can be an efficient and astute worker, but you also need a cut-off point that gives you the chance to pursue your own interests.

HORSE BONE

You are lively and imaginative and need freedom to express your ideas and emotions. Your interests are varied and you need to experiment before you commit yourself to a career or a relationship.

RAM BONE

It may take time for you to build stability in your life or for others to recognize your talents, but your independence and determination should be enough to carry you through the difficult times.

MONKEY BONE

You are alert and observant, reacting quickly to unexpected problems. You can spot opportunities in unlikely situations and sense potential trouble, but try not to be too impatient with others who do not share your alert nature.

ROOSTER BONE

You can be persuasive and enthusiastic, particularly when you have discovered a new interest or devised an original idea, and you reveal your thoughts with a natural charm and openness.

DOG BONE

You have an honest nature and rarely deceive others or betray confidences. You need peace to reflect and plan, and your ideas are often given support and encouragement from unexpected people.

PIG BONE

You have a straightforward and open nature that inspires trust. Luck is also on your side, and just when you need an opportunity someone or something usually turns up to help you.

NOBLE GOOD FORTUNE STARS

In the Three Lives system, stars are symbolized by people. Thus, the Chinese often refer to their Noble Star as their "noble man," since this is the star that reveals your skills and your fortune. The word "noble" has important connotations in Chinese tradition: it denotes learning, dignity, respect and influence, and consequently these stars give an indication of the strong points of your character.

There are seven Noble Good Fortune Stars, and in Chinese astrology there are also considered to be seven stars in the constellation of the Great Bear. These often appear in Chinese art, and play an important role in Taoist ritual. When only three of the seven stars are depicted, these symbolize the three wishes for long life, prosperity and happiness.

You may find that you come under the influence of more than one Noble Star, or that there are none at all in your horoscope. Do not worry if you fall into the latter category; this does not detract from your fortune since there are other stars which affect you.

To find out if any of the Noble Good Fortune Stars apply to you, you need to know your lunar month of birth and the Heavenly Stem for your day of birth. Both of these can be discovered by referring to the lunar chart on pages 118–27 (you will need to follow the instructions given in order to calculate your Heavenly Stem). Once you have done this, find your Heavenly Stem in the table below and then read down the column to find your lunar month – remember that there might not be a star that applies to your birth date. Alternatively, if your lunar month appears more than once in the column then there are several readings that apply to you: these indicate the various influences in your life. The row in which your lunar month lies denotes which Noble Star reading is yours.

HEAVENLY STEM FOR DAY OF BIRTH										NOBLE STAR
Chia	Yi	Ping	Ting	Mou	Chi	Keng	Hsin	Jen	Kuei	
6 10	8 10	8 10	8 10	6 10	4 10	6 10	1 5	3 4	4	T'ien Yi
1	12	1	11	7	6	5	4	3	12	Fu Hsing
8	1 7	10	10	2	1	5	4	5	4	T'ien Kuan
1	2	4	5	4	5	7	8	10	11	Ho Lu
2	3	5	6	7	1	8	9	10	11	Yang Jen
2	4	6	7	6	7	9	10	11	1	Chin Shen
8	11	11	1	2	1	5	4	5	4	Wen Hsing

LUNAR MONTH OF BIRTH

T'IEN YI

This is a prosperous and peaceful star, which forecasts financial stability and peaceful emotional relationships. It is also associated with property, and so you may have an interest in the construction, design or management of property.

FU HSING

Yin and yang are well-balanced in this star. You take the joys and disappointments of life in your stride, rarely suffering from depressed moods or emotional outbursts. Your stable nature is particularly effective in work connected to politics or public relations.

YANG JEN

This star reveals both independence and determination. There will be times when your plans are struck by setbacks or financial troubles, but persevere and the support you need will materialize in due course.

T'IEN KUAN

This star represents truth and generosity. You recognize the limits of your skills and are fair in business negotiations and financial dealings. Your creative skills might provide you with an unexpected source of income.

CHIN SHEN

This star represents intelligence and intuition. You observe the world around you and react quickly to unexpected crises or requests for help. You are alert to instructions and advice and recognize the level of action that is needed.

HO LU

This star reveals success built on efficient organization combined with good fortune. You are open to ideas and you plan carefully, and through luck or by good judgement your ideas are recognized and accepted.

WEN HSING

This is a creative and artistic star. You are stimulated by your surroundings and have a talent for identifying and developing unusual ideas, and these skills should serve you well in your career.

NINE STARS

The Nine Stars have wide-ranging associations beyond the realms of astrology. They correspond to the eight trigrams that are used in Chinese divination, plus the central point that is formed when the trigrams are placed in their traditional octagon-shaped sequence.

The trigrams are regarded as images of everything on earth and in heaven, and the central point is one of the five directions of a Chinese compass (the others being north, south, east and west).

The Nine Stars change their position every Chinese new year and, therefore, each new year (over a course of nine years) you belong to a different star. At the end of the nine-year period, you return to the star with which you began, and the cycle starts once more.

   The star that is shining on you this year depends on your age. You need to use the age that you were on the day the Chinese new year began (you can find all the new year dates listed on pages 10–11). Simply find your age in the table below and read across the line to find out the name of your star, then refer to the relevant reading to discover your forecast for this year.

AGE											STAR
0	9	18	27	36	45	54	63	72	81	90	Lo Hou
1	10	19	28	37	46	55	64	73	82	91	T'u Su
2	11	20	29	38	47	56	65	74	83	92	Shui Hsing
3	12	21	30	39	48	57	66	75	84	93	Chin Hsing
4	13	22	31	40	49	58	67	76	85	94	T'ai-yang
5	14	23	32	41	50	59	68	77	86	95	Huo Hsing
6	15	24	33	42	51	60	69	78	87	96	Chi Tu
7	16	25	34	43	52	61	70	79	88	97	T'ai-yin
8	17	26	35	44	53	62	71	80	89	98	Mu Hsing

LO HOU

This star casts a rather difficult shadow and you should plan carefully during the year to avoid accidents or litigation. Be sure to consider the circumstances and the people with whom you are dealing before you travel or become involved in negotiations.

T'U SU

This is an inauspicious star, but do not worry since it is unlikely that any serious problems will occur during the year. If you listen to advice and keep an open mind, your fortune will improve in the autumn and winter months.

HUO HSING

Handle your money carefully during the year and avoid any financial risks. Pay attention to your health and take the time to rest or pursue hobbies; if there are any warning signs that indicate ill health, make sure you do not ignore them.

SHUI HSING

There may be unexpected dangers or setbacks in the year ahead, so be prepared for change. Be honest in your dealings and sensitive to the needs of colleagues and friends during the course of the year, since their support may prove invaluable.

CHI TU

Your fortune in the spring and summer of this year is unpredictable, so do not take any unnecessary risks in relation to your health, family life or career. As the year moves into autumn and winter your fortune will improve and your concerns will be eased.

CHIN HSING

Pay attention to family affairs and avoid instigating quarrels this year. If you sense trouble brewing at home or at work you should act immediately to calm everyone down before circumstances grow out of control.

T'AI-YIN

This star casts an auspicious light on the year. There are signs of happiness and prosperity, and someone in a position of influence will be there to help you when you need support. If you have put effort into a project or scheme, you may reap the benefits from it this year.

T'AI-YANG

This is a lucky year for you, and any plans made in the past may now come to fruition. The good fortune associated with T'ai-Yang will enable you to acquire new property, land or goods. There is also an indication of a new birth in the family.

MU HSING

This is a highly auspicious star, indicating wealth, good fortune and happiness. You may hear good news or receive a surprise, and the good luck that this star brings should also affect your family. Do not worry about any minor ailments as they are unlikely to have long-term effects.

YEARLY GODS

In the Three Lives system, each of the Yearly Gods represents an aspect of astrology, fortune or life – hence the names such as Moon, Broken Year and Health, for example.

These gods are also often depicted as officials, with the head of an animal (one of the twelve animal signs) and the body of a human, wearing formal robes and holding a tablet containing the insignia of their imperial title of office.

The god changes every Chinese new year, and while some gods bring mixed fortune, others herald good luck throughout the year. Each year (over a course of twelve years), a different god affects your fortune, and at the end of the twelve-year period you return to the god with which you began, and the cycle repeats again.

    To find out which god is governing you this year, use the age that you were on the first day of the Chinese new year (see pages 10–11 for dates). Find your age in the table below and read across the line to see which forecast applies to you.

AGE									GOD
0	12	24	36	48	60	72	84		T'ai Sui
1	13	25	37	49	61	73	85		Sun
2	14	26	38	50	62	74	86		Ill-omened
3	15	27	39	51	63	75	87		Moon
4	16	28	40	52	64	76	88		Law
5	17	29	41	53	65	77	89		Health
6	18	30	42	54	66	78	90		Broken Year
7	19	31	43	55	67	79	91		Dragon Virtue
8	20	32	44	56	68	80	92		White Tiger
9	21	33	45	57	69	81	93		Fortune Virtue
10	22	34	46	58	70	82	94		Spirit
11	23	35	47	59	71	83	95		Sickness

T'AI SUI

T'ai Sui, the head of the gods, indicates that it may be hard to establish a balance between your personal life and working life this year. However, setbacks can be overcome if you consider commitments carefully.

SUN

This god brings luck throughout the year. You may discover that old relationships will be renewed and existing ones strengthened, and an idea or interest will be realized through the contacts you make.

ILL-OMENED

Do not take unnecessary financial risks during the year; trust your own judgement and intuition before agreeing to commitments or making promises. Take extra care with regard to your diet and general health.

MOON

This god brings good fortune to the home and heralds the birth of a child in your family. You should also be alert to unexpected personal opportunities throughout the year.

LAW

This god reveals an involvement with the law. You may find that you need to draw up a contract, seek legal advice or perhaps take a personal interest in someone else's legal affairs.

HEALTH

Take care of your health throughout the year since there is a sign of illness in this god. Cut back on excessive habits that might adversely affect your health and try to maintain a balanced diet.

BROKEN YEAR

Be cautious in negotiations and beware of investing money when the risks are high. There are, however, good indications for the health and security of your family during this year.

DRAGON VIRTUE

This is a promising year for planning or making journeys. There is also an indication of financial good fortune since this god forecasts money from an unexpected source.

WHITE TIGER

Be wary of investments that promise high returns or projects that appear to have strong potential. Check your facts carefully and seek objective advice before making any commitments.

FORTUNE VIRTUE

This promises to be a year of happy events. Projects or ideas that you have been considering may now be realized, strong relationships will be established and there may well be news of a birth in your family.

SPIRIT

Handle legal affairs carefully and check the background details of agreements or projects. There is the potential for arguments and misunderstandings to transpire, so beware of making sudden judgements.

SICKNESS

You may need to be patient and perseverant at the beginning of the year to avoid potential disagreements in later months. Do not be hasty in actions or decisions relating to your family.

TWELVE CREATURES

This method of divination is unique to the Three Lives system and includes animals that do not feature in any other area of Chinese astrology. In the original Three Lives book, it states that it is impossible to ascertain why or how this group of creatures came to be, although most of these animals are familiar figures in Chinese art or literature, and all have a special meaning in Chinese tradition.

For example, the lion is a powerful protector, the heron carries wishes for a happy journey through life, and the white crane symbolizes longevity and wisdom.

To see which creature is yours, you need to know your lunar month of birth (see pages 118–27) and the Earthly Branch for your year of birth (see the chart on page 61). Find your Earthly Branch in the table below, read down the column to find your lunar month and then read across to discover your creature.

| EARTHLY BRANCH FOR YEAR OF BIRTH | | | | | | | | | | | | |
Tzu	Chou	Yin	Mao	Chen	Szu	Wu	Wei	Shen	Yu	Hsu	Hai	CREATURE
1	2	3	4	5	6	7	8	9	10	11	12	Phoenix
2	3	4	5	6	7	8	9	10	11	12	1	Lion
3	4	5	6	7	8	9	10	11	12	1	2	Golden Pheasant
4	5	6	7	8	9	10	11	12	1	2	3	Mandarin Duck
5	6	7	8	9	10	11	12	1	2	3	4	Swallow
6	7	8	9	10	11	12	1	2	3	4	5	Heron
7	8	9	10	11	12	1	2	3	4	5	6	Stag
8	9	10	11	12	1	2	3	4	5	6	7	Peacock
9	10	11	12	1	2	3	4	5	6	7	8	Pigeon
10	11	12	1	2	3	4	5	6	7	8	9	Sparrow
11	12	1	2	3	4	5	6	7	8	9	10	Eagle
12	1	2	3	4	5	6	7	8	9	10	11	White Crane

LUNAR MONTH OF BIRTH

PHOENIX

You have a kind and thoughtful outlook and the support you offer others will not be forgotten. You are particularly suited to any profession connected with the law, since you analyze information carefully before making decisions.

LION

Your easygoing and relaxed manner allows you to form friendships with ease, and among these friends you are likely to make several influential contacts. You also seem to have a lucky streak that enables you to find a way out of difficulties.

GOLDEN PHEASANT

You are likely to have a natural flair for the arts and a talent for expressing yourself clearly. Try to develop these creative skills, since they could well provide you with a lucrative income.

MANDARIN DUCK

You may have a creative temperament, but the risks are likely to be high if you try to develop a career in the arts. You will probably be more successful working for a large company or governmental organization.

SWALLOW

You are intelligent and sharply observant but your straightforward approach may overwhelm others. Although you may be tempted to offer advice or correct faults, wait quietly for situations to resolve themselves.

HERON

You have a happy and enthusiastic approach to life, which helps to create a good working atmosphere. The decisions you make in your career may, however, give rise to disagreements within your family, but in time these differences will be reconciled.

STAG

Although you may already have a satisfactory occupation and stable income, part of you hankers after more money or status. Try to direct these energies away from work, towards personal relationships.

PEACOCK

You have a diligent and sensible attitude towards work, which will eventually reap rewards. You are able to deal with responsibility if limits have been established or if the job is within an organized hierarchy.

PIGEON

In your youth and your early twenties lucrative opportunities may slip away, regardless of the efforts you make. However, your patience should carry you through to far more prosperous years later on in life.

SPARROW

You enjoy the thrill of travel and the variety of experience it offers, and your ability to adapt helps you to relax in unknown places. However, your ties to your home are also strong and you are always likely to return to familiar ground.

EAGLE

You have a love of life, combined with an extravagant, exuberant and occasionally overpowering nature. Although you are an industrious worker your money is quickly spent, but this reading predicts a more prosperous old age.

WHITE CRANE

You are observant and creative, and are likely to have the potential for a successful artistic career. However, in order for your hopes or ideas to be realized you may find that you have to leave your home town or country.

CAREER STARS

The Career Stars reveal occupations and skills linked to your day and month of birth, and highlight the area where your "natural" talent lies. Therefore, each category name should not be taken literally.

Each star represents a traditional career in China. For example, careers in government administration were highly valued, and success in written exams opened the door to jobs in government service, encompassing the categories of Official, Scholar, Lecturer, Manager and Law and Order. The other occupations represented here traditionally played an important role in the smooth running of village and city life.

To find your Career Star, you need to know your lunar month of birth and the Heavenly Stem for your day of birth (see pages 118–27). Find your Heavenly Stem in the table below, read down the column until you come to your lunar month and then read across to find your star.

| HEAVENly STEM FOR DAY OF BIRTH | | | | | | | | | | CAREER STAR |
Chia	Yi	Ping	Ting	Mou	Chi	Keng	Hsin	Jen	Kuei	
1	2	3	4	5	6	7	8	9	10	Official
2	3	4	5	6	7	8	9	10	11	Butcher
3	4	5	6	7	8	9	10	11	12	Scholar
4	5	6	7	8	9	10	11	12	1	Blacksmith
5	6	7	8	9	10	11	12	1	2	Lecturer
6	7	8	9	10	11	12	1	2	3	Manager
7	8	9	10	11	12	1	2	3	4	Musician
8	9	10	11	12	1	2	3	4	5	Herbalist
9	10	11	12	1	2	3	4	5	6	Monk
10	11	12	1	2	3	4	5	6	7	Tailor
11	12	1	2	3	4	5	6	7	8	Law & Order
12	1	2	3	4	5	6	7	8	9	Craftsman

LUNAR MONTH OF BIRTH

MANAGER

This is a star linked to organization and prosperity. You are likely to have natural leadership qualities and are a good judge of situations and character.

MUSICIAN

This star is associated with adaptability and wisdom. You have a wide variety of talents and approach projects with perception and enthusiasm.

OFFICIAL

This is a prosperous and wealthy star that reveals creative skills in the fields of art or design, but also has strong links with literature.

HERBALIST

This star is linked to health and medicinal herbs and plants. It reveals an interest in diet, exercise, physical activity or general health matters, making you suited to work in health-related professions.

BUTCHER

This is a star of practical skills, and you are most suited to work that requires planning, common sense and dexterity.

MONK

This is a star of reflection, meditation or contemplation. You are suited to a creative job that allows you freedom to express your ideas or gives you the independence to travel.

SCHOLAR

This star represents writers and artists, and you are suited to a wide variety of creative jobs that require fresh and unusual ideas.

TAILOR

This star is associated with design and indicates an interest in colors, patterns and materials, which makes you best suited to detailed or practical work.

BLACKSMITH

This star is linked with practical and physical work, and you are likely to have the application and concentration to deal with demanding tasks.

LAW AND ORDER

This star is linked to careers in law, the armed forces, the police or the government and reveals a talent for direct, practical work that offers you responsibility and authority.

LECTURER

This star guides teachers, officials and administrators and reveals natural skills for conveying information or developing schemes.

CRAFTSMAN

This star is associated with crafts, building and manufacture. You have a wide variety of practical skills and enjoy working with materials that can be used in design or construction.

LUNAR CHART 1936-2031

The information given on the following pages includes lunar equivalents for solar dates between 1936 and 2031. It enables you to discover your lunar month of birth, your lunar day of birth, your number in the sixty-year cycle and the Heavenly Stem for your day of birth.

You will need to know the details above in order to calculate a number of the readings featured in this book. Each year in the chart includes the following information:

- **The number of the year in the sixty-year cycle**
- **The solar dates equivalent to each lunar month**
- **The Heavenly Stem for the day on which the lunar month begins**

You will be able to discover your lunar month of birth and your number in the sixty-year cycle straight away by referring to the information given for your year of birth. But in order to calculate your lunar day of birth and the Heavenly Stem for your day of birth you will need to follow the instructions outlined below.

CALCULATING YOUR LUNAR DAY OF BIRTH

Look up your year of birth in the chart (see pages 120–27) and check the day on which your lunar month begins. Then, find this day in the grid shown to the right and, counting this as day one, count off the number of days to your birthday: this will give you your lunar day of birth. Remember that some months only have thirty days, so, when applicable, you should count to 30 in the grid and then return to 1 to continue counting. In the case of February, leap years are marked in the chart so that you know whether to count to 28 or 29 before returning to 1 (see key on pages 120–27). Also, do not forget that in the lunar calendar an extra month is "added" to make a double month every two or three years (see "The Lunar Calendar" on page 8). The double months are

highlighted in the chart for information purposes only: you calculate your lunar day of birth in the same way as you would for any other month.

Read the two examples given below to help you to make sure that you have calculated your lunar day of birth correctly.

1	2	3	4	5	6	7	8
9	10	11	12	13	14	15	16
17	18	19	20	21	22	23	24
25	26	27	28	29	30	31	

EXAMPLE ONE

If you were born on 26 July 1942, your birthday falls in the lunar month beginning on 13 July. Find 13 in the grid and then, counting this day as number one, count through the days until you come to your birthday (you must count your birthday as the final day). Your lunar day of birth, therefore, is 14.

EXAMPLE TWO

If you were born on 19 March 1960, your birthday falls in the lunar month beginning on 27 February. Find 27 in the grid and then, counting this day as the first day, count through the days up to – and including – your birthday. Remember that you must count up to 29 on the grid before going back to 1, as 1960 was a leap year. Your lunar day of birth is 22.

CALCULATING THE HEAVENLY STEM FOR YOUR DAY OF BIRTH

Once you have calculated your lunar day of birth, you can then use this number to work out your Heavenly Stem. First, you must check which Heavenly Stem corresponds to the first day of your lunar month (this is the Heavenly Stem listed next to your lunar month in the chart). Then you simply find it in the list shown in the "Sequence of Heavenly Stems" box (see right) and, using the number of your lunar day of birth, count through the list to find the Heavenly Stem for your day of birth.

Read the examples given below to make sure you have calculated your Heavenly Stem correctly.

EXAMPLE ONE

If you were born on 26 July 1942, your birthday falls in the lunar month beginning on 13 July. The Heavenly Stem for 13 July is *Ting*, and you have already calculated your lunar day of birth as 14. Find *Ting* in the list and, counting it as number one, count through the list until you have counted off fourteen Heavenly Stems. The Heavenly Stem for your day of birth is *Keng*.

EXAMPLE TWO

If you were born on 19 March 1960, your birthday falls in the lunar month beginning on 27 February. The Heavenly Stem for 27 February is *Yi*, and you have already calculated your lunar day of birth as 22. Find *Yi* in the list and, counting it as the first Heavenly Stem, count through the list until you have counted off twenty-two Heavenly Stems. The Heavenly Stem for your day of birth is *Ping*.

SEQUENCE OF HEAVENLY STEMS

The Heavenly Stems always repeat in sequence, so when you get to the end of the list you sim ply go back to the beginning to continue counting.

CHIA	CHIA
YI	YI
PING	PING
TING	TING
MOU	MOU
CHI	CHI
KENG	KENG
HSIN	HSIN
JEN	JEN
KUEI	KUEI

*1936 Number in the sixty-year cycle: 13

SOLAR DATES	LUNAR MONTH	HEAVENLY STEM
Jan 24 – Feb 22	1	Yi
Feb 23 – March 22	2	Yi
March 23 – April 20	3	Chia
April 21 – May 20	3	Kuei
May 21 – June 18	4	Kuei
June 19 – July 17	5	Jen
July 18 – Aug 16	6	Hsin
Aug 17 – Sept 15	7	Hsin
Sept 16 – Oct 14	8	Hsin
Oct 15 – Nov 13	9	Keng
Nov 14 – Dec 13	10	Keng
Dec 14 – Jan 12 1937	11	Keng
Jan 13 – Feb 10	12	Keng

1937 Number in the sixty-year cycle: 14

SOLAR DATES	LUNAR MONTH	HEAVENLY STEM
Feb 11 – March 12	1	Chi
March 13 – April 10	2	Chi
April 11 – May 9	3	Mou
May 10 – June 8	4	Ting
June 9 – July 7	5	Ting
July 8 – Aug 5	6	Ping
Aug 6 – Sept 4	7	Yi
Sept 5 – Oct 3	8	Yi
Oct 4 – Nov 2	9	Chia
Nov 3 – Dec 2	10	Chia
Dec 3 – Jan 1 1938	11	Chia
Jan 2 – Jan 30	12	Chia

1938 Number in the sixty-year cycle: 15

SOLAR DATES	LUNAR MONTH	HEAVENLY STEM
Jan 31 – March 1	1	Kuei
March 2 – March 31	2	Kuei
April 1 – April 29	3	Kuei
April 30 – May 28	4	Jen
May 29 – June 27	5	Hsin
June 28 – July 26	6	Hsin
July 27 – Aug 24	7	Keng
Aug 25 – Sept 23	7	Chi
Sept 24 – Oct 22	8	Chi
Oct 23 – Nov 21	9	Mou
Nov 22 – Dec 21	10	Mou
Dec 22 – Jan 19 1939	11	Mou
Jan 20 – Feb 18	12	Ting

1939 Number in the sixty-year cycle: 16

SOLAR DATES	LUNAR MONTH	HEAVENLY STEM
Feb 19 – March 20	1	Ting
March 21 – April 19	2	Ting
April 20 – May 18	3	Ting
May 19 – June 16	4	Ping
June 17 – July 16	5	Yi
July 17 – Aug 14	6	Yi
Aug 15 – Sept 12	7	Chia
Sept 13 – Oct 12	8	Kuei
Oct 13 – Nov 10	9	Kuei
Nov 11 – Dec 10	10	Jen
Dec 11 – Jan 8 1940	11	Jen
Jan 9 – Feb 7	12	Hsin

*1940 Number in the sixty-year cycle: 17

SOLAR DATES	LUNAR MONTH	HEAVENLY STEM
Feb 8 – March 8	1	Hsin
March 9 – April 7	2	Hsin
April 8 – May 6	3	Hsin
May 7 – June 5	4	Keng
June 6 – July 4	5	Keng
July 5 – Aug 3	6	Chi
Aug 4 – Sept 1	7	Chi
Sept 2 – Sept 30	8	Mou
Oct 1 – Oct 30	9	Ting
Oct 31 – Nov 28	10	Ting
Nov 29 – Dec 28	11	Ping
Dec 29 – Jan 26 1941	12	Ping

1941 Number in the sixty-year cycle: 18

SOLAR DATES	LUNAR MONTH	HEAVENLY STEM
Jan 27 – Feb 25	1	Yi
Feb 26 – March 27	2	Yi
March 28 – April 25	3	Yi
April 26 – May 25	4	Chia
May 26 – June 24	5	Chia
June 25 – July 23	6	Chia
July 24 – Aug 22	6	Kuei
Aug 23 – Sept 20	7	Kuei
Sept 21 – Oct 19	8	Jen
Oct 20 – Nov 18	9	Hsin
Nov 19 – Dec 17	10	Hsin
Dec 18 – Jan 16 1942	11	Keng
Jan 17 – Feb 14	12	Keng

1942 Number in the sixty-year cycle: 19

SOLAR DATES	LUNAR MONTH	HEAVENLY STEM
Feb 15 – March 16	1	Chi
March 17 – April 14	2	Chi
April 15 – May 14	3	Mou
May 15 – June 13	4	Mou
June 14 – July 12	5	Mou
July 13 – Aug 11	6	Ting
Aug 12 – Sept 9	7	Ting
Sept 10 – Oct 9	8	Ping
Oct 10 – Nov 7	9	Ping
Nov 8 – Dec 7	10	Yi
Dec 8 – Jan 5 1943	11	Yi
Jan 6 – Feb 4	12	Chia

1943 Number in the sixty-year cycle: 20

SOLAR DATES	LUNAR MONTH	HEAVENLY STEM
Feb 5 – March 5	11	Chia
March 6 – April 4	2	Kuei
April 5 – May 3	3	Kuei
May 4 – June 2	4	Jen
June 3 – July 1	5	Jen
July 2 – July 31	6	Hsin
Aug 1 – Aug 30	7	Hsin
Aug 31 – Sept 28	8	Hsin
Sept 29 – Oct 28	9	Keng
Oct 29 – Nov 26	10	Keng
Nov 27 – Dec 26	11	Chi
Dec 27 – Jan 24 1944	12	Chi

*1944 Number in the sixty-year cycle: 21

SOLAR DATES	LUNAR MONTH	HEAVENLY STEM
Jan 25 – Feb 23	1	Mou
Feb 24 – March 23	2	Mou
March 24 – April 22	3	Ting
April 23 – May 21	4	Ting
May 22 – June 20	4	Ping
June 21 – July 19	5	Ping
July 20 – Aug 18	6	Yi
Aug 19 – Sept 16	7	Yi
Sept 17 – Oct 16	8	Chia
Oct 17 – Nov 15	9	Chia
Nov 16 – Dec 14	10	Chia
Dec 15 – Jan 13 1945	11	Kuei
Jan 14 – Feb 12	12	Kuei

1945 Number in the sixty-year cycle: 22

SOLAR DATES	LUNAR MONTH	HEAVENLY STEM
Feb 13 – March 13	1	Kuei
March 14 – April 11	2	Jen
April 12 – May 11	3	Hsin
May 12 – June 9	4	Hsin
June 10 – July 8	5	Keng
July 9 – Aug 7	6	Chi
Aug 8 – Sept 5	7	Chi
Sept 6 – Oct 5	8	Mou
Oct 6 – Nov 4	9	Mou
Nov 5 – Dec 4	10	Mou
Dec 5 – Jan 2 1946	11	Mou
Jan 3 – Feb 1	12	Ting

1946 Number in the sixty-year cycle: 23

SOLAR DATES	LUNAR MONTH	HEAVENLY STEM
Feb 2 – March 3	1	Ting
March 4 – April 1	2	Ting
April 2 – April 30	3	Ping
May 1 – May 30	4	Yi
May 31 – June 28	5	Yi
June 29 – July 27	6	Chia
July 28 – Aug 26	7	Kuei
Aug 27 – Sept 24	8	Kuei
Sept 25 – Oct 24	9	Jen
Oct 25 – Nov 23	10	Jen
Nov 24 – Dec 22	11	Jen
Dec 23 – Jan 21 1947	12	Hsin

1947 Number in the sixty-year cycle: 24

SOLAR DATES	LUNAR MONTH	HEAVENLY STEM
Jan 22 – Feb 20	1	Hsin
Feb 21 – March 22	2	Hsin
March 23 – April 20	2	Hsin
April 21 – May 19	3	Keng
May 20 – June 18	4	Chi
June 19 – July 17	5	Chi
July 18 – Aug 15	6	Mou
Aug 16 – Sept 14	7	Ting
Sept 15 – Oct 13	8	Ting
Oct 14 – Nov 12	9	Ping
Nov 13 – Dec 11	10	Ping
Dec 12 – Jan 10 1948	11	Yi
Jan 11 – Feb 9	12	Yi

*1948 Number in the sixty-year cycle: 25

SOLAR DATES	LUNAR MONTH	HEAVENLY STEM
Feb 10 – March 10	1	Yi
March 11 – April 8	2	Yi
April 9 – May 8	3	Chia
May 9 – June 6	4	Chia
June 7 – July 6	5	Kuei
July 7 – Aug 4	6	Kuei
Aug 7 – Sept 2	7	Jen
Sept 3 – Oct 2	8	Hsin
Oct 3 – Oct 31	9	Hsin
Nov 1 – Nov 30	10	Keng
Dec 1 – Dec 29	11	Keng
Dec 30 – Jan 28 1949	12	Chi

*1952 Number in the sixty-year cycle: 29

SOLAR DATES	LUNAR MONTH	HEAVENLY STEM
Jan 27 – Feb 24	1	Jen
Feb 25 – March 25	2	Hsin
March 26 – April 23	3	Hsin
April 24 – May 23	4	Keng
May 24 – June 21	5	Keng
June 22 – July 21	5	Chi
July 22 – Aug 19	6	Chi
Aug 20 – Sept 18	7	Mou
Sept 19 – Oct 18	8	Mou
Oct 19 – Nov 16	9	Mou
Nov 17 – Dec 16	10	Ting
Dec 17 – Jan 14 1953	11	Ting
Jan 15 – Feb 13	12	Ping

*1956 Number in the sixty-year cycle: 33

SOLAR DATES	LUNAR MONTH	HEAVENLY STEM
Feb 12 – March 11	1	Ting
March 12 – April 10	2	Mou
April 11 – May 9	3	Mou
May 10 – June 8	4	Ting
June 9 – July 7	5	Ting
July 8 – Aug 5	6	Ping
Aug 6 – Sept 4	7	Yi
Sept 5 – Oct 3	8	Yi
Oct 4 – Nov 2	9	Chia
Nov 3 – Dec 1	10	Chia
Dec 2 – Dec 31	11	Kuei
Jan 1 1957 – Jan 30	12	Kuei

1949 Number in the sixty-year cycle: 26

SOLAR DATES	LUNAR MONTH	HEAVENLY STEM
Jan 29 – Feb 27	1	Chi
Feb 28 – March 28	2	Chi
March 29 – April 27	3	Mou
April 28 – May 27	4	Mou
May 28 – June 25	5	Mou
June 26 – July 25	6	Ting
July 26 – Aug 23	7	Ting
Aug 24 – Sept 21	7	Ping
Sept 22 – Oct 21	8	Yi
Oct 22 – Nov 19	9	Yi
Nov 20 – Dec 19	10	Chia
Dec 20 – Jan 17 1950	11	Chia
Jan 18 – Feb 16	12	Kuei

1953 Number in the sixty-year cycle: 30

SOLAR DATES	LUNAR MONTH	HEAVENLY STEM
Feb 14 – March 14	1	Ping
March 15 – April 13	2	Yi
April 14 – May 12	3	Yi
May 13 – June 10	4	Chia
June 11 – July 10	5	Kuei
July 11 – Aug 9	6	Kuei
Aug 10 – Sept 7	7	Kuei
Sept 8 – Oct 7	8	Jen
Oct 8 – Nov 6	9	Jen
Nov 7 – Dec 5	10	Jen
Dec 6 – Jan 4 1954	11	Hsin
Jan 5 – Feb 2	12	Hsin

1957 Number in the sixty-year cycle: 34

SOLAR DATES	LUNAR MONTH	HEAVENLY STEM
Jan 31 – March 1	1	Kuei
March 2 – March 30	2	Kuei
March 31 – April 29	3	Jen
April 30 – May 28	4	Jen
May 29 – June 27	5	Hsin
June 28 – July 26	6	Hsin
July 27 – Aug 24	7	Keng
Aug 25 – Sept 23	8	Chi
Sept 24 – Oct 22	8	Chi
Oct 23 – Nov 21	9	Mou
Nov 22 – Dec 20	10	Mou
Dec 21 – Jan 19 1958	11	Ting
Jan 20 – Feb 17	12	Ting

1950 Number in the sixty-year cycle: 27

SOLAR DATES	LUNAR MONTH	HEAVENLY STEM
Feb 17 – March 17	1	Kuei
March 18 – April 16	2	Jen
April 17 – May 16	3	Jen
May 17 – June 14	4	Jen
June 15 – July 14	5	Hsin
July 15 – Aug 13	6	Hsin
Aug 14 – Sept 11	7	Hsin
Sept 12 – Oct 10	8	Keng
Oct 11 – Nov 9	9	Chi
Nov 10 – Dec 8	10	Chi
Dec 9 – Jan 7 1951	11	Mou
Jan 8 – Feb 5	12	Mou

1954 Number in the sixty-year cycle: 31

SOLAR DATES	LUNAR MONTH	HEAVENLY STEM
Feb 3 – March 4	1	Keng
March 5 – April 2	2	Keng
April 3 – May 2	3	Chi
May 3 – May 31	4	Chi
June 1 – June 29	5	Mou
June 30 – July 29	6	Ting
July 30 – Aug 27	7	Ting
Aug 28 – Sept 26	8	Ping
Sept 27 – Oct 26	9	Ping
Oct 27 – Nov 24	10	Ping
Nov 25 – Dec 24	11	Yi
Dec 25 – Jan 23 1955	12	Yi

1958 Number in the sixty-year cycle: 35

SOLAR DATES	LUNAR MONTH	HEAVENLY STEM
Feb 18 – March 19	1	Ping
March 20 – April 18	2	Ping
April 19 – May 18	3	Ping
May 19 – June 16	4	Ping
June 17 – July 16	5	Yi
July 17 – Aug 14	6	Yi
Aug 15 – Sept 12	7	Chia
Sept 13 – Oct 12	8	Kuei
Oct 13 – Nov 10	9	Kuei
Nov 11 – Dec 10	10	Jen
Dec 11 – Jan 8 1959	11	Jen
Jan 9 – Feb 7	12	Hsin

1951 Number in the sixty-year cycle: 28

SOLAR DATES	LUNAR MONTH	HEAVENLY STEM
Feb 6 – March 7	1	Ting
March 8 – April 5	2	Ting
April 6 – May 5	3	Ping
May 6 – June 4	4	Ping
June 5 – July 3	5	Ping
July 4 – Aug 2	6	Yi
Aug 3 – Aug 31	7	Yi
Sept 1 – Sept 30	8	Chia
Oct 1 – Oct 29	9	Chia
Oct 30 – Nov 28	10	Kuei
Nov 29 – Dec 27	11	Kuei
Dec 28 – Jan 26 1952	12	Jen

1955 Number in the sixty-year cycle: 32

SOLAR DATES	LUNAR MONTH	HEAVENLY STEM
Jan 24 – Feb 21	1	Yi
Feb 22 – March 23	2	Chia
March 24 – April 21	3	Chia
April 22 – May 21	3	Kuei
May 22 – June 19	4	Kuei
June 20 – July 18	5	Jen
July 19 – Aug 17	6	Hsin
Aug 18 – Sept 15	7	Hsin
Sept 16 – Oct 15	8	Keng
Oct 16 – Nov 13	9	Keng
Nov 14 – Dec 13	10	Chi
Dec 14 – Jan 12 1956	11	Chi
Jan 13 – Feb 11	12	Chi

1959 Number in the sixty-year cycle: 36

SOLAR DATES	LUNAR MONTH	HEAVENLY STEM
Feb 8 – March 8	1	Hsin
March 9 – April 7	2	Keng
April 8 – May 7	3	Keng
May 8 – June 5	4	Keng
June 6 – July 5	5	Chi
July 6 – Aug 3	6	Chi
Aug 4 – Sept 2	7	Mou
Sept 3 – Oct 1	8	Mou
Oct 2 – Oct 31	9	Ting
Nov 1 – Nov 29	10	Ting
Nov 30 – Dec 29	11	Ping
Dec 30 – Jan 27 1960	12	Ping

*1960 Number in the sixty-year cycle: 37

SOLAR DATES	LUNAR MONTH	HEAVENLY STEM
Jan 28 – Feb 26	1	Yi
Feb 27 – March 26	2	Yi
March 27 – April 25	3	Chia
April 26 – May 24	4	Chia
May 25 – June 23	5	Kuei
June 24 – July 23	6	Kuei
July 24 – Aug 21	6	Kuei
Aug 22 – Sept 20	7	Jen
Sept 21 – Oct 19	8	Jen
Oct 20 – Nov 18	9	Hsin
Nov 19 – Dec 17	10	Hsin
Dec 18 – Jan 16 1961	11	Keng
Jan 17 – Feb 14	12	Keng

1961 Number in the sixty-year cycle: 38

SOLAR DATES	LUNAR MONTH	HEAVENLY STEM
Feb 15 – March 16	1	Chi
March 17 – April 14	2	Chi
April 15 – May 14	3	Mou
May 15 – June 12	4	Mou
June 13 – July 12	5	Ting
July 13 – Aug 10	6	Ting
Aug 11 – Sept 9	7	Ping
Sept 10 – Oct 9	8	Ping
Oct 10 – Nov 7	9	Ping
Nov 8 – Dec 7	10	Yi
Dec 8 – Jan 5 1962	11	Yi
Jan 6 – Feb 4	12	Chia

1962 Number in the sixty-year cycle: 39

SOLAR DATES	LUNAR MONTH	HEAVENLY STEM
Feb 5 – March 5	1	Chia
March 6 – April 4	2	Kuei
April 5 – May 3	3	Kuei
May 4 – June 1	4	Jen
June 2 – July 1	5	Hsin
July 2 – July 30	6	Hsin
July 31 – Aug 29	7	Keng
Aug 30 – Sept 28	8	Keng
Sept 29 – Oct 27	9	Keng
Oct 28 – Nov 26	10	Chi
Nov 27 – Dec 26	11	Chi
Dec 27 – Jan 24 1963	12	Chi

1963 Number in the sixty-year cycle: 40

SOLAR DATES	LUNAR MONTH	HEAVENLY STEM
Jan 25 – Feb 23	1	Mou
Feb 24 – March 24	2	Mou
March 25 – April 23	3	Ting
April 24 – May 22	4	Ting
May 23 – June 20	4	Ping
June 21 – July 20	5	Yi
July 21 – Aug 18	6	Yi
Aug 19 – Sept 17	7	Chia
Sept 18 – Oct 16	8	Chia
Oct 17 – Nov 15	9	Kuei
Nov 16 – Dec 15	10	Kuei
Dec 16 – Jan 14 1964	11	Kuei
Jan 15 – Feb 12	12	Kuei

*1964 Number in the sixty-year cycle: 41

SOLAR DATES	LUNAR MONTH	HEAVENLY STEM
Feb 13 – March 13	1	Jen
March 14 – April 11	2	Jen
April 12 – May 11	3	Hsin
May 12 – June 9	4	Hsin
June 10 – July 8	5	Keng
July 9 – Aug 7	6	Chi
Aug 8 – Sept 5	7	Chi
Sept 6 – Oct 5	8	Mou
Oct 6 – Nov 3	9	Mou
Nov 4 – Dec 3	10	Ting
Dec 4 – Jan 2 1965	11	Ting
Jan 3 – Feb 1	12	Ting

1965 Number in the sixty-year cycle: 42

SOLAR DATES	LUNAR MONTH	HEAVENLY STEM
Feb 2 – March 2	1	Ting
March 3 – April 1	2	Ping
April 2 – April 30	3	Ping
May 1 – May 30	4	Yi
May 31 – June 28	5	Yi
June 29 – July 27	6	Chia
July 28 – Aug 26	7	Kuei
Aug 27 – Sept 24	8	Kuei
Sept 25 – Oct 23	9	Jen
Oct 24 – Nov 22	10	Hsin
Nov 23 – Dec 22	11	Hsin
Dec 23 – Jan 20 1966	12	Hsin

1966 Number in the sixty-year cycle: 43

SOLAR DATES	LUNAR MONTH	HEAVENLY STEM
Jan 21 – Feb 19	1	Keng
Feb 20 – March 21	2	Keng
March 22 – April 20	3	Keng
April 21 – May 19	3	Keng
May 20 – June 18	4	Chi
June 19 – July 17	5	Chi
July 18 – Aug 15	6	Mou
Aug 16 – Sept 14	7	Ting
Sept 15 – Oct 13	8	Ting
Oct 14 – Nov 11	9	Ping
Nov 12 – Dec 11	10	Yi
Dec 12 – Jan 10 1967	11	Yi
Jan 11 – Feb 8	12	Yi

1967 Number in the sixty-year cycle: 44

SOLAR DATES	LUNAR MONTH	HEAVENLY STEM
Feb 9 – March 10	1	Chia
March 11 – April 9	2	Chia
April 10 – May 8	3	Chia
May 9 – June 7	4	Kuei
June 8 – July 7	5	Kuei
July 8 – Aug 5	6	Kuei
Aug 6 – Sept 3	7	Jen
Sept 4 – Oct 3	8	Hsin
Oct 4 – Nov 1	9	Hsin
Nov 2 – Dec 1	10	Keng
Dec 2 – Dec 30	11	Keng
Dec 31 – Jan 29 1968	12	Chi

*1968 Number in the sixty-year cycle: 45

SOLAR DATES	LUNAR MONTH	HEAVENLY STEM
Jan 30 – Feb 27	1	Chi
Feb 28 – March 28	2	Mou
March 29 – April 26	3	Mou
April 27 – May 26	4	Ting
May 27 – June 25	5	Ting
June 26 – July 24	6	Ting
July 25 – Aug 23	7	Ping
Aug 24 – Sept 21	7	Ping
Sept 22 – Oct 21	8	Yi
Oct 22 – Nov 19	9	Yi
Nov 20 – Dec 19	10	Chia
Dec 20 – Jan 17 1969	11	Chia
Jan 18 – Feb 16	12	Kuei

1969 Number in the sixty-year cycle: 46

SOLAR DATES	LUNAR MONTH	HEAVENLY STEM
Feb 17 – March 17	1	Kuei
March 18 – April 16	2	Jen
April 17 – May 15	3	Jen
May 16 – June 14	4	Hsin
June 15 – July 13	5	Hsin
July 14 – Aug 12	6	Keng
Aug 13 – Sept 11	7	Keng
Sept 12 – Oct 10	8	Keng
Oct 11 – Nov 9	9	Mou
Nov 10 – Dec 8	10	Chi
Dec 9 – Jan 7 1970	11	Mou
Jan 8 – Feb 5	12	Mou

1970 Number in the sixty-year cycle: 47

SOLAR DATES	LUNAR MONTH	HEAVENLY STEM
Feb 6 – March 7	1	Ting
March 8 – April 5	2	Ting
April 6 – May 4	3	Ping
May 5 – June 3	4	Yi
June 4 – July 2	5	Yi
July 3 – Aug 1	6	Chia
Aug 2 – Aug 31	7	Chia
Sept 1 – Sept 29	8	Chia
Sept 30 – Oct 29	9	Kuei
Oct 30 – Nov 28	10	Kuei
Nov 29 – Dec 27	11	Kuei
Dec 28 – Jan 26 1971	12	Jen

1971 Number in the sixty-year cycle: 48

SOLAR DATES	LUNAR MONTH	HEAVENLY STEM
Jan 27 – Feb 24	1	Jen
Feb 25 – March 26	2	Hsin
March 27 – April 24	3	Hsin
April 25 – May 23	4	Keng
May 24 – June 22	5	Chi
June 23 – July 21	5	Chi
July 22 – Aug 20	6	Mou
Aug 21 – Sept 18	7	Mou
Sept 19 – Oct 18	8	Ting
Oct 19 – Nov 17	9	Ting
Nov 18 – Dec 17	10	Ting
Dec 18 – Jan 15 1972	11	Ting
Jan 16 – Feb 14	12	Ping

*1972 Number in the sixty-year cycle: 49

SOLAR DATES	LUNAR MONTH	HEAVENLY STEM
Feb 15 – March 14	1	Ping
March 15 – April 13	2	Yi
April 14 – May 12	3	Yi
May 13 – June 10	4	Chia
June 11 – July 10	5	Kuei
July 11 – Aug 8	6	Kuei
Aug 9 – Sept 7	7	Jen
Sept 8 – Oct 6	8	Jen
Oct 7 – Nov 5	9	Hsin
Nov 6 – Dec 5	10	Hsin
Dec 6 – Jan 3 1973	11	Hsin
Jan 4 – Feb 2	12	Keng

*1976 Number in the sixty-year cycle: 53

SOLAR DATES	LUNAR MONTH	HEAVENLY STEM
Jan 31 – Feb 29	1	Jen
March 1 – March 30	2	Jen
March 31 – April 28	3	Jen
April 29 – May 28	4	Hsin
May 29 – June 26	5	Hsin
June 27 – July 26	6	Keng
July 27 – Aug 24	7	Keng
Aug 25 – Sept 23	8	Chi
Sept 24 – Oct 22	8	Chi
Oct 23 – Nov 20	9	Mou
Nov 21 – Dec 20	10	Ting
Dec 21 – Jan 18 1977	11	Ting
Jan 19 – Feb 17	12	Ping

*1980 Number in the sixty-year cycle: 57

SOLAR DATES	LUNAR MONTH	HEAVENLY STEM
Feb 16 – March 16	1	Chi
March 17 – April 14	2	Chi
April 15 – May 13	3	Mou
May 14 – June 12	4	Ting
June 13 – July 11	5	Ting
July 12 – Aug 10	6	Ping
Aug 11 – Sept 8	7	Ping
Sept 9 – Oct 8	8	Yi
Oct 9 – Nov 7	9	Yi
Nov 8 – Dec 6	10	Yi
Dec 7 – Jan 5 1981	11	Chia
Jan 6 – Feb 4	12	Chia

1973 Number in the sixty-year cycle: 50

SOLAR DATES	LUNAR MONTH	HEAVENLY STEM
Feb 3 – March 4	1	Keng
March 5 – April 2	2	Keng
April 3 – May 2	3	Chi
May 3 – May 31	4	Chi
June 1 – June 29	5	Mou
June 30 – July 29	6	Ting
July 30 – Aug 27	7	Ting
Aug 28 – Sept 25	8	Ping
Sept 26 – Oct 25	9	Yi
Oct 26 – Nov 24	10	Yi
Nov 25 – Dec 23	11	Yi
Dec 24 – Jan 22 1974	12	Chia

1977 Number in the sixty-year cycle: 54

SOLAR DATES	LUNAR MONTH	HEAVENLY STEM
Feb 18 – March 19	1	Ping
March 20 – April 17	2	Ping
April 18 – May 17	3	Yi
May 18 – June 16	4	Yi
June 17 – July 15	5	Yi
July 16 – Aug 14	6	Chia
Aug 15 – Sept 12	7	Chia
Sept 13 – Oct 12	8	Kuei
Oct 13 – Nov 10	9	Kuei
Nov 11 – Dec 10	10	Jen
Dec 11 – Jan 8 1978	11	Jen
Jan 9 – Feb 6	12	Hsin

1981 Number in the sixty-year cycle: 58

SOLAR DATES	LUNAR MONTH	HEAVENLY STEM
Feb 5 – March 5	1	Chia
March 6 – April 4	2	Kuei
April 5 – May 3	3	Kuei
May 4 – June 1	4	Jen
June 2 – July 1	5	Hsin
July 2 – July 30	6	Hsin
July 31 – Aug 28	7	Keng
Aug 29 – Sept 27	8	Chi
Sept 28 – Oct 27	9	Chi
Oct 28 – Nov 25	10	Chi
Nov 26 – Dec 25	11	Mou
Dec 26 – Jan 24 1982	12	Mou

1974 Number in the sixty-year cycle: 51

SOLAR DATES	LUNAR MONTH	HEAVENLY STEM
Jan 23 – Feb 21	1	Chia
Feb 22 – March 23	2	Chia
March 24 – April 21	3	Chia
April 22 – May 21	4	Kuei
May 22 – June 19	4	Kuei
June 20 – July 19	5	Jen
July 20 – Aug 17	6	Hsin
Aug 18 – Sept 15	7	Hsin
Sept 16 – Oct 14	8	Keng
Oct 15 – Nov 13	9	Chi
Nov 14 – Dec 13	10	Chi
Dec 14 – Jan 11 1975	11	Chi
Jan 12 – Feb 10	12	Mou

1978 Number in the sixty-year cycle: 55

SOLAR DATES	LUNAR MONTH	HEAVENLY STEM
Feb 7 – March 8	1	Keng
March 9 – April 6	2	Keng
April 7 – May 6	3	Chi
May 7 – June 5	4	Chi
June 6 – July 4	5	Chi
July 5 – Aug 3	6	Mou
Aug 4 – Sept 2	7	Mou
Sept 3 – Oct 1	8	Mou
Oct 2 – Oct 31	9	Ting
Nov 1 – Nov 29	10	Ting
Nov 30 – Dec 29	11	Ping
Dec 30 – Jan 27 1979	12	Ping

1982 Number in the sixty-year cycle: 59

SOLAR DATES	LUNAR MONTH	HEAVENLY STEM
Jan 25 – Feb 23	1	Mou
Feb 24 – March 24	2	Mou
March 25 – April 23	3	Ting
April 24 – May 22	4	Ting
May 23 – June 20	4	Ping
June 21 – July 20	5	Yi
July 21 – Aug 18	6	Yi
Aug 19 – Sept 16	7	Chia
Sept 17 – Oct 16	8	Kuei
Oct 17 – Nov 14	9	Kuei
Nov 15 – Dec 14	10	Jen
Dec 15 – Jan 13 1983	11	Jen
Jan 14 – Feb 12	12	Jen

1975 Number in the sixty-year cycle: 52

SOLAR DATES	LUNAR MONTH	HEAVENLY STEM
Feb 11 – March 12	1	Mou
March 13 – April 11	2	Mou
April 12 – May 10	3	Mou
May 11 – June 9	4	Ting
June 10 – July 8	5	Ting
July 9 – Aug 6	6	Ping
Aug 7 – Sept 5	7	Yi
Sept 6 – Oct 4	8	Yi
Oct 5 – Nov 2	9	Chia
Nov 3 – Dec 2	10	Kuei
Dec 3 – Dec 31 1976	11	Kuei
Jan 1 1976 – Jan 30	12	Jen

1979 Number in the sixty-year cycle: 56

SOLAR DATES	LUNAR MONTH	HEAVENLY STEM
Jan 28 – Feb 26	1	Yi
Feb 27 – March 27	2	Yi
March 28 – April 25	3	Chia
April 26 – May 25	4	Kuei
May 26 – June 23	5	Kuei
June 24 – July 23	6	Jen
July 24 – Aug 22	6	Jen
Aug 23 – Sept 20	7	Jen
Sept 21 – Oct 20	8	Hsin
Oct 21 – Nov 19	9	Hsin
Nov 20 – Dec 18	10	Hsin
Dec 19 – Jan 17 1980	11	Keng
Jan 18 – Feb 15	12	Keng

1983 Number in the sixty-year cycle: 60

SOLAR DATES	LUNAR MONTH	HEAVENLY STEM
Feb 13 – March 14	1	Jen
March 15 – April 12	2	Jen
April 13 – May 12	3	Hsin
May 13 – June 10	4	Hsin
June 11 – July 9	5	Keng
July 10 – Aug 8	6	Chi
Aug 9 – Sept 6	7	Chi
Sept 7 – Oct 5	8	Mou
Oct 6 – Nov 4	9	Ting
Nov 5 – Dec 3	10	Ting
Dec 4 – Jan 2 1984	11	Ping
Jan 3 – Feb 1	12	Ping

*1984 Number in the sixty-year cycle: 1

SOLAR DATES	LUNAR MONTH	HEAVENLY STEM
Feb 2 – March 2	1	Ping
March 3 – March 31	2	Ping
April 1 – April 30	3	Yi
May 1 – May 30	4	Yi
May 31 – June 28	5	Yi
June 29 – July 27	6	Chia
July 28 – Aug 26	7	Kuei
Aug 27 – Sept 24	8	Kuei
Sept 25 – Oct 23	9	Jen
Oct 24 – Nov 22	10	Hsin
Nov 23 – Dec 21	10	Hsin
Dec 22 – Jan 20 1985	11	Keng
Jan 21 – Feb 19	12	Keng

1985 Number in the sixty-year cycle: 2

SOLAR DATES	LUNAR MONTH	HEAVENLY STEM
Feb 20 – March 20	1	Keng
March 21 – April 19	2	Chi
April 20 – May 19	3	Chi
May 20 – June 17	4	Chi
June 18 – July 17	5	Mou
July 18 – Aug 15	6	Mou
Aug 16 – Sept 14	7	Ting
Sept 15 – Oct 13	8	Ting
Oct 14 – Nov 11	9	Ping
Nov 12 – Dec 11	10	Yi
Dec 12 – Jan 9 1986	11	Yi
Jan 10 – Feb 8	12	Chia

1986 Number in the sixty-year cycle: 3

SOLAR DATES	LUNAR MONTH	HEAVENLY STEM
Feb 9 – March 9	1	Chia
March 10 – April 8	2	Kuei
April 9 – May 8	3	Kuei
May 9 – June 6	4	Kuei
June 7 – July 7	5	Jen
July 8 – Aug 5	6	Hsin
Aug 6 – Sept 3	7	Jen
Sept 4 – Oct 3	8	Hsin
Oct 4 – Nov 1	9	Hsin
Nov 2 – Dec 1	10	Keng
Dec 2 – Dec 30	11	Keng
Dec 31 – Jan 28 1987	12	Chi

1987 Number in the sixty-year cycle: 4

SOLAR DATES	LUNAR MONTH	HEAVENLY STEM
Jan 29 – Feb 27	1	Mou
Feb 28 – March 28	2	Mou
March 29 – April 27	3	Ping
April 28 – May 26	4	Ting
May 27 – June 25	5	Ping
June 26 – July 25	6	Ping
July 26 – Aug 23	6	Ping
Aug 24 – Sept 22	7	Yi
Sept 23 – Oct 22	8	Yi
Oct 23 – Nov 20	9	Yi
Nov 21 – Dec 20	10	Chia
Dec 21 – Jan 18 1988	11	Chia
Jan 19 – Feb 16	12	Kuei

*1988 Number in the sixty-year cycle: 5

SOLAR DATES	LUNAR MONTH	HEAVENLY STEM
Feb 17 – March 17	1	Jen
March 18 – April 15	2	Jen
April 16 – May 15	3	Hsin
May 16 – June 13	4	Hsin
June 14 – July 13	5	Keng
July 14 – Aug 11	6	Keng
Aug 12 – Sept 10	7	Chi
Sept 11 – Oct 10	8	Chi
Oct 11 – Nov 8	9	Chi
Nov 9 – Dec 8	10	Mou
Dec 9 – Jan 7 1989	11	Mou
Jan 8 – Feb 5	12	Mou

1989 Number in the sixty-year cycle: 6

SOLAR DATES	LUNAR MONTH	HEAVENLY STEM
Feb 6 – March 7	1	Ting
March 8 – April 5	2	Ting
April 6 – May 4	3	Ping
May 5 – June 3	4	Yi
June 4 – July 2	5	Yi
July 3 – July 31	6	Chia
Aug 1 – Aug 30	7	Kuei
Aug 31 – Sept 29	8	Kuei
Sept 30 – Oct 28	9	Kuei
Oct 29 – Nov 27	10	Jen
Nov 28 – Dec 27	11	Jen
Dec 28 – Jan 26 1990	12	Jen

1990 Number in the sixty-year cycle: 7

SOLAR DATES	LUNAR MONTH	HEAVENLY STEM
Jan 27 – Feb 24	1	Jen
Feb 25 – March 26	2	Hsin
March 27 – April 24	3	Hsin
April 25 – May 23	4	Keng
May 24 – June 22	5	Chi
June 23 – July 21	5	Chi
July 22 – Aug 19	6	Mou
Aug 20 – Sept 18	7	Ting
Sept 19 – Oct 17	8	Ting
Oct 18 – Nov 16	9	Ping
Nov 17 – Dec 16	10	Ping
Dec 17 – Jan 15 1991	11	Ping
Jan 16 – Feb 14	12	Ping

1991 Number in the sixty-year cycle: 8

SOLAR DATES	LUNAR MONTH	HEAVENLY STEM
Feb 15 – March 15	1	Ping
March 16 – April 14	2	Yi
April 15 – May 13	3	Yi
May 14 – June 11	4	Chia
June 12 – July 11	5	Kuei
July 12 – Aug 9	6	Kuei
Aug 10 – Sept 7	7	Jen
Sept 8 – Oct 7	8	Hsin
Oct 8 – Nov 5	9	Hsin
Nov 6 – Dec 5	10	Keng
Dec 6 – Jan 4 1992	11	Keng
Jan 5 – Feb 3	12	Keng

*1992 Number in the sixty-year cycle: 9

SOLAR DATES	LUNAR MONTH	HEAVENLY STEM
Feb 4 – March 3	1	Keng
March 4 – April 2	2	Chi
April 3 – May 2	3	Chi
May 3 – May 31	4	Chi
June 1 – June 29	5	Mou
June 30 – July 29	6	Ting
July 30 – Aug 27	7	Ting
Aug 28 – Sept 25	8	Ping
Sept 26 – Oct 25	9	Yi
Oct 26 – Nov 23	10	Yi
Nov 24 – Dec 23	11	Chia
Dec 24 – Jan 22 1993	12	Chia

1993 Number in the sixty-year cycle: 10

SOLAR DATES	LUNAR MONTH	HEAVENLY STEM
Jan 23 – Feb 20	1	Chia
Feb 21 – March 22	2	Kuei
March 23 – April 21	3	Kuei
April 22 – May 20	3	Kuei
May 21 – June 18	4	Jen
June 20 – July 18	5	Jen
July 19 – Aug 17	6	Hsin
Aug 18 – Sept 15	7	Hsin
Sept 16 – Oct 14	8	Keng
Oct 15 – Nov 13	9	Chi
Nov 14 – Dec 12	10	Chi
Dec 13 – Jan 11 1994	11	Ting
Jan 12 – Feb 9	12	Mou

1994 Number in the sixty-year cycle: 11

SOLAR DATES	LUNAR MONTH	HEAVENLY STEM
Feb 10 – March 11	1	Ting
March 12 – April 10	2	Ting
April 11 – May 10	3	Ting
May 11 – June 8	4	Ting
June 9 – July 8	5	Ping
July 9 – Aug 6	6	Ping
Aug 7 – Sept 5	7	Yi
Sept 6 – Oct 4	8	Yi
Oct 5 – Nov 2	9	Chia
Nov 3 – Dec 2	10	Kuei
Dec 3 – Dec 31	11	Kuei
Jan 1 1995 – Jan 30	12	Jen

1995 Number in the sixty-year cycle: 12

SOLAR DATES	LUNAR MONTH	HEAVENLY STEM
Jan 31 – Feb 28	1	Jen
March 1 – March 30	2	Hsin
March 31 – April 29	3	Hsin
April 30 – May 28	4	Hsin
May 29 – June 27	5	Keng
June 28 – July 26	6	Keng
July 27 – Aug 25	7	Chi
Aug 26 – Sept 24	8	Chi
Sept 25 – Oct 23	8	Chi
Oct 24 – Nov 21	9	Mou
Nov 22 – Dec 21	10	Ting
Dec 22 – Jan 19 1996	11	Ting
Jan 20 – Feb 18	12	Ping

*1996 Number in the sixty-year cycle: 13

SOLAR DATES	LUNAR MONTH	HEAVENLY STEM
Feb 19 – March 18	1	Ping
March 19 – April 17	2	Yi
April 18 – May 16	3	Yi
May 17 – June 15	4	Chia
June 16 – July 15	5	Chia
July 16 – Aug 13	6	Chia
Aug 14 – Sept 12	7	Kuei
Sept 13 – Oct 11	8	Kuei
Oct 12 – Nov 10	9	Jen
Nov 11 – Dec 10	10	Jen
Dec 11 – Jan 8 1997	11	Jen
Jan 9 – Feb 6	12	Hsin

*2000 Number in the sixty-year cycle: 17

SOLAR DATES	LUNAR MONTH	HEAVENLY STEM
Feb 5 – March 5	1	Kuei
March 6 – April 4	2	Kuei
April 5 – May 3	3	Kuei
May 4 – June 1	4	Jen
June 2 – July 1	5	Hsin
July 2 – July 30	6	Hsin
July 31 – Aug 28	7	Keng
Aug 29 – Sept 27	8	Chi
Sept 28 – Oct 26	9	Chi
Oct 27 – Nov 25	10	Mou
Nov 26 – Dec 25	11	Mou
Dec 26 – Jan 23 2001	12	Mou

*2004 Number in the sixty-year cycle: 21

SOLAR DATES	LUNAR MONTH	HEAVENLY STEM
Jan 22 – Feb 19	1	Keng
Feb 20 – March 20	2	Chi
March 21 – April 18	2	Chi
April 19 – May 18	3	Mou
May 19 – June 17	4	Mou
June 18 – July 16	5	Mou
July 17 – Aug 15	6	Ting
Aug 16 – Sept 13	7	Ting
Sept 14 – Oct 13	8	Ping
Oct 14 – Nov 11	9	Ping
Nov 12 – Dec 11	10	Yi
Dec 12 – Jan 9 2005	11	Yi
Jan 10 – Feb 8	12	Chia

1997 Number in the sixty-year cycle: 14

SOLAR DATES	LUNAR MONTH	HEAVENLY STEM
Feb 7 – March 8	1	Keng
March 9 – April 6	2	Keng
April 7 – May 6	3	Chi
May 7 – June 4	4	Chi
June 5 – July 4	5	Mou
July 5 – Aug 2	6	Mou
Aug 3 – Sept 1	7	Ting
Sept 2 – Oct 1	8	Ting
Oct 2 – Oct 30	9	Ting
Oct 31 – Nov 29	10	Ping
Nov 30 – Dec 29	11	Ping
Dec 30 – Jan 27 1998	12	Ping

2001 Number in the sixty-year cycle: 18

SOLAR DATES	LUNAR MONTH	HEAVENLY STEM
Jan 24 – Feb 22	1	Ting
Feb 23 – March 24	2	Ting
March 25 – April 22	3	Ting
April 23 – May 22	4	Ping
May 23 – June 20	4	Ping
June 21 – July 20	5	Yi
July 21 – Aug 18	6	Yi
Aug 19 – Sept 16	7	Chia
Sept 17 – Oct 16	8	Kuei
Oct 17 – Nov 14	9	Kuei
Nov 15 – Dec 14	10	Jen
Dec 15 – Jan 12 2002	11	Jen
Jan 13 – Feb 11	12	Hsin

2005 Number in the sixty-year cycle: 22

SOLAR DATES	LUNAR MONTH	HEAVENLY STEM
Feb 9 – March 9	1	Chia
March 10 – April 8	2	Kuei
April 9 – May 7	3	Kuei
May 8 – June 6	4	Hsin
June 7 – July 5	5	Jen
July 6 – Aug 4	6	Hsin
Aug 5 – Sept 3	7	Hsin
Sept 4 – Oct 2	8	Hsin
Oct 3 – Nov 1	9	Keng
Nov 2 – Nov 30	10	Keng
Dec 1 – Dec 30	11	Chi
Dec 31 – Jan 28 2006	12	Chi

1998 Number in the sixty-year cycle: 15

SOLAR DATES	LUNAR MONTH	HEAVENLY STEM
Jan 28 – Feb 26	1	Yi
Feb 27 – March 27	2	Yi
March 28 – April 25	3	Chia
April 26 – May 25	4	Kuei
May 26 – June 23	5	Kuei
June 24 – July 22	5	Jen
July 23 – Aug 21	6	Hsin
Aug 22 – Sept 20	7	Hsin
Sept 21 – Oct 19	8	Hsin
Oct 20 – Nov 18	9	Keng
Nov 19 – Dec 18	10	Keng
Dec 19 – Jan 16 1999	11	Keng
Jan 17 – Feb 15	12	Chi

2002 Number in the sixty-year cycle: 19

SOLAR DATES	LUNAR MONTH	HEAVENLY STEM
Feb 12 – March 13	1	Hsin
March 14 – April 12	2	Hsin
April 13 – May 11	3	Hsin
May 12 – June 10	4	Keng
June 11 – July 9	5	Keng
July 10 – Aug 8	6	Chi
Aug 9 – Sept 6	7	Chi
Sept 7 – Oct 5	8	Mou
Oct 6 – Nov 4	9	Ting
Nov 5 – Dec 3	10	Ting
Dec 4 – Jan 2 2003	11	Ping
Jan 3 – Jan 31	12	Ping

2006 Number in the sixty-year cycle: 23

SOLAR DATES	LUNAR MONTH	HEAVENLY STEM
Jan 19 – Feb 27	1	Mou
Feb 28 – March 28	2	Mou
March 29 – April 27	3	Ting
April 28 – May 26	4	Ting
May 27 – June 25	5	Ping
June 26 – July 24	6	Ping
July 25 – Aug 23	7	Yi
Aug 24 – Sept 21	7	Yi
Sept 22 – Oct 21	8	Chia
Oct 22 – Nov 20	9	Chia
Nov 21 – Dec 19	10	Chia
Dec 20 – Jan 18 2007	11	Kuei
Jan 19 – Feb 17	12	Kuei

1999 Number in the sixty-year cycle: 16

SOLAR DATES	LUNAR MONTH	HEAVENLY STEM
Feb 16 – March 17	1	Chi
March 18 – April 15	2	Chi
April 16 – May 14	3	Mou
May 15 – June 13	4	Ting
June 14 – July 12	5	Ting
July 13 – Aug 10	6	Ping
Aug 11 – Sept 9	7	Yi
Sept 10 – Oct 8	8	Yi
Oct 9 – Nov 7	9	Chia
Nov 8 – Dec 7	10	Chia
Dec 8 – Jan 6 2000	11	Chia
Jan 7 – Feb 4	12	Chia

2003 Number in the sixty-year cycle: 20

SOLAR DATES	LUNAR MONTH	HEAVENLY STEM
Feb 1 – March 2	1	Yi
March 3 – April 1	2	Yi
April 2 – April 30	3	Yi
May 1 – May 30	4	Chia
May 31 – June 29	5	Chia
June 30 – July 28	6	Chia
July 29 – Aug 27	7	Kuei
Aug 28 – Sept 25	8	Kuei
Sept 26 – Oct 24	9	Jen
Oct 25 – Nov 23	10	Hsin
Nov 24 – Dec 22	11	Hsin
Dec 23 – Jan 21 2004	12	Keng

2007 Number in the sixty-year cycle: 24

SOLAR DATES	LUNAR MONTH	HEAVENLY STEM
Feb 18 – March 18	1	Kuei
March 19 – April 16	2	Jen
April 17 – May 16	3	Hsin
May 17 – June 14	4	Hsin
June 15 – July 13	5	Keng
July 14 – Aug 12	6	Chi
Aug 13 – Sept 10	7	Chi
Sept 11 – Oct 10	8	Mou
Oct 11 – Nov 9	9	Mou
Nov 10 – Dec 9	10	Mou
Dec 10 – Jan 7 2008	11	Mou
Jan 8 – Feb 6	12	Ting

*2008 Number in the sixty-year cycle: 25

SOLAR DATES	LUNAR MONTH	HEAVENLY STEM
Feb 7 – March 7	1	Ting
March 8 – April 5	2	Ting
April 6 – May 4	3	Ping
May 5 – June 3	4	Yi
June 4 – July 2	5	Yi
July 3 – July 31	6	Chia
Aug 1 – Aug 30	7	Kuei
Aug 31 – Sept 28	8	Kuei
Sept 29 – Oct 28	9	Jen
Oct 29 – Nov 27	10	Jen
Nov 28 – Dec 26	11	Jen
Dec 27 – Jan 25 2009	12	Hsin

2009 Number in the sixty-year cycle: 26

SOLAR DATES	LUNAR MONTH	HEAVENLY STEM
Jan 26 – Feb 24	1	Hsin
Feb 25 – March 26	2	Hsin
March 27 – April 24	3	Hsin
April 25 – May 23	4	Keng
May 24 – June 22	5	Chi
June 23 – July 21	5	Chi
July 22 – Aug 19	6	Mou
Aug 20 – Sept 18	7	Ting
Sept 19 – Oct 17	8	Ting
Oct 18 – Nov 16	9	Ping
Nov 17 – Dec 15	10	Ping
Dec 16 – Jan 14 2010	11	Yi
Jan 15 – Feb 13	12	Yi

2010 Number in the sixty-year cycle: 27

SOLAR DATES	LUNAR MONTH	HEAVENLY STEM
Feb 14 – March 15	1	Yi
March 16 – April 13	2	Yi
April 14 – May 13	3	Chia
May 14 – June 11	4	Chia
June 12 – July 11	5	Kuei
July 12 – Aug 9	6	Kuei
Aug 10 – Sept 7	7	Jen
Sept 8 – Oct 7	8	Hsin
Oct 8 – Nov 5	9	Hsin
Nov 6 – Dec 5	10	Keng
Dec 6 – Jan 3 2011	11	Keng
Jan 4 – Feb 2	12	Chi

2011 Number in the sixty-year cycle: 28

SOLAR DATES	LUNAR MONTH	HEAVENLY STEM
Feb 3 – March 4	1	Chi
March 5 – April 2	2	Chi
April 3 – May 2	3	Mou
May 3 – June 1	4	Mou
June 2 – June 30	5	Mou
July 1 – July 30	6	Ting
July 31 – Aug 28	7	Ting
Aug 29 – Sept 26	8	Ping
Sept 27 – Oct 26	9	Yi
Oct 27 – Nov 24	10	Yi
Nov 25 – Dec 24	11	Chia
Dec 25 – Jan 22 2012	12	Chia

*2012 Number in the sixty-year cycle: 29

SOLAR DATES	LUNAR MONTH	HEAVENLY STEM
Jan 23 – Feb 21	1	Kuei
Feb 22 – March 21	2	Kuei
March 22 – April 20	3	Jen
April 21 – May 20	4	Jen
May 21 – June 18	4	Jen
June 19 – July 18	5	Hsin
July 19 – Aug 16	6	Hsin
Aug 17 – Sept 15	7	Keng
Sept 16 – Oct 14	8	Keng
Oct 15 – Nov 13	9	Chi
Nov 14 – Dec 12	10	Chi
Dec 13 – Jan 11 2013	11	Mou
Jan 12 – Feb 9	12	Mou

2013 Number in the sixty-year cycle: 30

SOLAR DATES	LUNAR MONTH	HEAVENLY STEM
Feb 10 – March 11	1	Ting
March 12 – April 9	2	Ting
April 10 – May 9	3	Ping
May 10 – June 7	4	Ping
June 8 – July 7	5	Yi
July 8 – Aug 6	6	Yi
Aug 7 – Sept 4	7	Yi
Sept 5 – Oct 4	8	Chia
Oct 5 – Nov 2	9	Chia
Nov 3 – Dec 2	10	Kuei
Dec 3 – Dec 31	11	Kuei
Jan 1 2014 – Jan 30	12	Jen

2014 Number in the sixty-year cycle: 31

SOLAR DATES	LUNAR MONTH	HEAVENLY STEM
Jan 31 – Feb 28	1	Jen
March 1 – March 30	2	Hsin
March 31 – April 28	3	Hsin
April 29 – May 28	4	Keng
May 29 – June 26	5	Keng
June 27 – July 26	6	Chi
July 27 – Aug 24	7	Chi
Aug 25 – Sept 23	8	Mou
Sept 24 – Oct 23	9	Mou
Oct 24 – Nov 21	9	Mou
Nov 22 – Dec 21	10	Ting
Dec 22 – Jan 19 2015	11	Ting
Jan 20 – Feb 18	12	Ping

2015 Number in the sixty-year cycle: 32

SOLAR DATES	LUNAR MONTH	HEAVENLY STEM
Feb 19 – March 19	1	Ping
March 20 – April 18	2	Yi
April 19 – May 17	3	Yi
May 18 – June 15	4	Chia
June 16 – July 15	5	Kuei
July 16 – Aug 13	6	Kuei
Aug 14 – Sept 12	7	Jen
Sept 13 – Oct 12	8	Jen
Oct 13 – Nov 11	9	Jen
Nov 12 – Dec 10	10	Jen
Dec 11 – Jan 9 2016	11	Hsin
Jan 10 – Feb 7	12	Hsin

*2016 Number in the sixty-year cycle: 33

SOLAR DATES	LUNAR MONTH	HEAVENLY STEM
Feb 8 – March 8	1	Keng
March 9 – April 6	2	Keng
April 7 – May 6	3	Chi
May 7 – June 4	4	Chi
June 5 – July 3	5	Mou
July 4 – Aug 2	6	Ting
Aug 3 – Aug 31	7	Ting
Sept 1 – Sept 30	8	Ping
Oct 1 – Oct 30	9	Ping
Oct 31 – Nov 28	10	Ping
Nov 29 – Dec 28	11	Yi
Dec 29 – Jan 27 2017	12	Yi

2017 Number in the sixty-year cycle: 34

SOLAR DATES	LUNAR MONTH	HEAVENLY STEM
Jan 28 – Feb 25	1	Yi
Feb 26 – March 27	2	Chia
March 28 – April 25	3	Chia
April 26 – May 25	4	Kuei
May 26 – June 23	5	Kuei
June 24 – July 22	6	Jen
July 23 – Aug 21	6	Hsin
Aug 22 – Sept 19	7	Hsin
Sept 20 – Oct 19	8	Keng
Oct 20 – Nov 17	9	Keng
Nov 18 – Dec 17	10	Chi
Dec 18 – Jan 16 2018	11	Chi
Jan 17 – Feb 15	12	Chi

2018 Number in the sixty-year cycle: 35

SOLAR DATES	LUNAR MONTH	HEAVENLY STEM
Feb 16 – March 16	1	Chi
March 17 – April 15	2	Mou
April 16 – May 14	3	Mou
May 15 – June 13	4	Ting
June 14 – July 12	5	Ting
July 13 – Aug 10	6	Ping
Aug 11 – Sept 9	7	Yi
Sept 10 – Oct 8	8	Yi
Oct 9 – Nov 7	9	Chia
Nov 8 – Dec 6	10	Chia
Dec 7 – Jan 5 2019	11	Kuei
Jan 6 – Feb 4	12	Kuei

2019 Number in the sixty-year cycle: 36

SOLAR DATES	LUNAR MONTH	HEAVENLY STEM
Feb 5 – March 6	1	Kuei
March 7 – April 4	2	Kuei
April 5 – May 4	3	Jen
May 5 – June 2	4	Jen
June 3 – July 2	5	Hsin
July 3 – July 31	6	Hsin
Aug 1 – Aug 29	7	Keng
Aug 30 – Sept 28	8	Chi
Sept 29 – Oct 27	9	Chi
Oct 28 – Nov 25	10	Mou
Nov 26 – Dec 25	11	Ting
Dec 26 – Jan 24 2020	12	Ting

*2020 Number in the sixty-year cycle: 37

SOLAR DATES	LUNAR MONTH	HEAVENLY STEM
Jan 25 – Feb 22	1	Ting
Feb 23 – March 23	2	Ping
March 24 – April 22	3	Ping
April 23 – May 22	4	Ping
May 23 – June 20	4	Ping
June 21 – July 20	5	Yi
July 21 – Aug 18	6	Yi
Aug 19 – Sept 16	7	Chia
Sept 17 – Oct 16	8	Kuei
Oct 17 – Nov 14	9	Kuei
Nov 15 – Dec 14	10	Jen
Dec 15 – Jan 12 2021	11	Jen
Jan 13 – Feb 11	12	Hsin

2021 Number in the sixty-year cycle: 38

SOLAR DATES	LUNAR MONTH	HEAVENLY STEM
Feb 12 – March 12	1	Hsin
March 13 – April 11	2	Keng
April 12 – May 11	3	Keng
May 12 – June 9	4	Keng
June 10 – July 9	5	Chi
July 10 – Aug 7	6	Chi
Aug 8 – Sept 6	7	Mou
Sept 7 – Oct 5	8	Mou
Oct 6 – Nov 4	9	Ting
Nov 5 – Dec 3	10	Ting
Dec 4 – Jan 2 2022	11	Ping
Jan 3 – Jan 31	12	Ping

2022 Number in the sixty-year cycle: 39

SOLAR DATES	LUNAR MONTH	HEAVENLY STEM
Feb 1 – March 2	1	Yi
March 3 – March 31	2	Yi
April 1 – April 30	3	Chia
May 1 – May 29	4	Chia
May 30 – June 28	5	Kuei
June 29 – July 28	6	Jen
July 29 – Aug 26	7	Jen
Aug 27 – Sept 25	8	Hsin
Sept 26 – Oct 24	9	Hsin
Oct 25 – Nov 23	10	Keng
Nov 24 – Dec 22	11	Keng
Dec 23 – Jan 21 2023	12	Chi

2023 Number in the sixty-year cycle: 40

SOLAR DATES	LUNAR MONTH	HEAVENLY STEM
Jan 22 – Feb 19	1	Chi
Feb 20 – March 21	2	Mou
March 22 – April 19	2	Mou
April 20 – May 18	3	Ting
May 19 – June 17	4	Ping
June 18 – July 17	5	Ping
July 18 – Aug 15	6	Ping
Aug 16 – Sept 14	7	Yi
Sept 15 – Oct 14	8	Yi
Oct 15 – Nov 12	9	Yi
Nov 13 – Dec 12	10	Chia
Dec 13 – Jan 10 2024	11	Chia
Jan 11 – Feb 9	12	Kuei

*2024 Number in the sixty-year cycle: 41

SOLAR DATES	LUNAR MONTH	HEAVENLY STEM
Feb 10 – March 9	1	Kuei
March 10 – April 8	2	Jen
April 9 – May 7	3	Jen
May 8 – June 5	4	Hsin
June 6 – July 5	5	Keng
July 6 – Aug 3	6	Keng
Aug 4 – Sept 2	7	Chi
Sept 3 – Oct 2	8	Chi
Oct 3 – Oct 31	9	Chi
Nov 1 – Nov 30	10	Mou
Dec 1 – Dec 30	11	Mou
Dec 31 – Jan 28 2025	12	Mou

2025 Number in the sixty-year cycle: 42

SOLAR DATES	LUNAR MONTH	HEAVENLY STEM
Jan 29 – Feb 27	1	Ting
Feb 28 – March 28	2	Ting
March 29 – April 27	3	Ping
April 28 – May 26	4	Ping
May 27 – June 24	5	Yi
June 25 – July 24	6	Chia
July 25 – Aug 22	6	Chia
Aug 23 – Sept 21	7	Kuei
Sept 22 – Oct 20	8	Kuei
Oct 21 – Nov 19	9	Jen
Nov 20 – Dec 19	10	Jen
Dec 20 – Jan 18 2026	11	Jen
Jan 19 – Feb 16	12	Jen

2026 Number in the sixty-year cycle: 43

SOLAR DATES	LUNAR MONTH	HEAVENLY STEM
Feb 17 – March 18	1	Hsin
March 19 – April 16	2	Hsin
April 17 – May 16	3	Keng
May 17 – June 14	4	Keng
June 15 – July 13	5	Chi
July 14 – Aug 12	6	Mou
Aug 13 – Sept 10	7	Mou
Sept 11 – Oct 9	8	Ting
Oct 10 – Nov 8	9	Ping
Nov 9 – Dec 8	10	Ping
Dec 9 – Jan 7 2027	11	Ping
Jan 8 – Feb 5	12	Ping

2027 Number in the sixty-year cycle: 44

SOLAR DATES	LUNAR MONTH	HEAVENLY STEM
Feb 6 – March 7	1	Yi
March 8 – April 6	2	Yi
April 7 – May 6	3	Yi
May 7 – June 4	4	Yi
June 5 – July 3	5	Chia
July 4 – Aug 1	6	Kuei
Aug 2 – Aug 31	7	Jen
Sept 1 – Sept 29	8	Jen
Sept 30 – Oct 28	9	Hsin
Oct 29 – Nov 27	10	Keng
Nov 28 – Dec 27	11	Keng
Dec 28 – Jan 25 2028	12	Keng

*2028 Number in the sixty-year cycle: 45

SOLAR DATES	LUNAR MONTH	HEAVENLY STEM
Jan 26 – Feb 24	1	Chi
Feb 25 – March 25	2	Chi
March 26 – April 24	3	Chi
April 25 – May 23	4	Chi
May 24 – June 22	5	Mou
June 23 – July 21	5	Mou
July 22 – Aug 19	6	Ting
Aug 20 – Sept 18	7	Ping
Sept 19 – Oct 17	8	Ping
Oct 18 – Nov 15	9	Yi
Nov 16 – Dec 15	10	Chia
Dec 16 – Jan 14 2029	11	Chia
Jan 15 – Feb 12	12	Chia

2029 Number in the sixty-year cycle: 46

SOLAR DATES	LUNAR MONTH	HEAVENLY STEM
Feb 13 – March 14	1	Kuei
March 15 – April 13	2	Kuei
April 14 – May 12	3	Kuei
May 13 – June 11	4	Jen
June 12 – July 10	5	Jen
July 11 – Aug 9	6	Hsin
Aug 10 – Sept 7	7	Hsin
Sept 8 – Oct 7	8	Keng
Oct 8 – Nov 5	9	Keng
Nov 6 – Dec 4	10	Chi
Dec 5 – Jan 3 2030	11	Mou
Jan 4 – Feb 2	12	Mou

2030 Number in the sixty-year cycle: 47

SOLAR DATES	LUNAR MONTH	HEAVENLY STEM
Feb 3 – March 3	1	Mou
March 4 – April 2	2	Ting
April 3 – May 1	3	Ting
May 2 – May 31	4	Ping
June 1 – June 30	5	Ping
July 1 – July 29	6	Ping
July 30 – Aug 28	7	Yi
Aug 29 – Sept 26	8	Yi
Sept 27 – Oct 26	9	Chia
Oct 27 – Nov 24	10	Chia
Nov 25 – Dec 24	11	Kuei
Dec 25 – Jan 22 2031	12	Kuei

2031 Number in the sixty-year cycle: 48

SOLAR DATES	LUNAR MONTH	HEAVENLY STEM
Jan 23 – Feb 20	1	Jen
Feb 21 – March 22	2	Hsin
March 23 – April 21	3	Hsin
April 22 – May 20	3	Hsin
May 21 – June 19	4	Keng
June 20 – July 18	5	Keng
July 19 – Aug 17	6	Chi
Aug 18 – Sept 16	7	Chi
Sept 17 – Oct 15	8	Chi
Oct 16 – Nov 14	9	Mou
Nov 15 – Dec 13	10	Mou
Dec 14 – Jan 12 2032	11	Ting
Jan 13 – Feb 10	12	Ting

FURTHER READING

The books below offer a useful introduction to aspects of Chinese divinational arts, myths and legends, and Taoist beliefs.

Kwok, Man-Ho, *The Feng Shui Kit: The Chinese Way to Health, Wealth and Happiness, at Home and at Work*. Edited by Joanne O'Brien. Boston, MA: Charles E. Tuttle Co., Inc., 1995

Kwok, Man-Ho and Joanne O'Brien, *The Eight Immortals of Taoism: Legends and Fables of Popular Taosim*. Introduction by Martin Palmer. New York: Meridian, 1991

Kwok, Man-Ho, Martin Palmer and Jay Ramsay, *Tao Te Ching*. Rockport, MA: Element Books, 1993

Palmer, Martin, *The Elements of Taoism*. Rockport, MA: Element Books, 1991

Palmer, Martin, *Yin and Yang: Understanding the Chinese Philosophy of Opposites and How to Apply it to Your Everyday Life*. London: Piatkus, 1997

Palmer, Martin, Jay Ramsay and Zhao Xiaomin (translators), *I Ching: The Shamanic Oracle of Change*. San Francisco, CA: Thorsons, 1995

Palmer, Martin and Zhao Xiaomin, *Essential Chinese Mythology*. San Francisco, CA: Thorsons, 1997

PICTURE CREDITS

Cover tristan tan/ShutterStockphoto.Inc

ShutterStockphoto.Inc 1, 2-3, 4-5, 6-7, 10-11, 12, 14, 16, 18, 20, 22, 24, 26, 28, 30, 32, 34, 36, 58, 62t, 63t, 64t, 65t, 66t, 67t, 68t, 69t, 70t, 71t, 72t, 73t, 74, 80, 105 tristan tan; 9, 107 IrinaKrivoruchko

13, 15, 17, 19, 21, 23, 25, 27, 29, 31, 33, 35, 38 to 57, 62b, 63b, 64b, 65b, 66b, 67b, 68b, 69b, 70b, 71b, 72b, 73b, 80, 82, 84, 86, 88, 90, 92, 94, 96, 98, 100, 102, 118-19 Claire Melinsky

All other images supplied by The Noun Project (thenounproject.com)

Eddison Books Limited

Creative Consultant Nick Eddison
Managing Editor Tessa Monina
Design Jane McKenna (www.fogdog.co.uk)
Editorial John Andrews
Production Sarah Rooney & Cara Clapham

Original text edited by Joanne O'Brien